Grade 5
Poetry
Comprehension Skills

Contents

Poetry: Grade 5, SV 9895-7

Grade 5
Poetry Comprehension Skills

Introduction

This book is designed to help students become better readers through the reading of poetry. The IRA/NCTE Standards for the English Language Arts list as the first recommendation: "Students read a wide range of print and nonprint texts to build an understanding of texts, of themselves, and of the cultures of the United States and the world…." Poetry is a form of literature easily read and enjoyed by students of all ages. Children's books often use the rhythm and rhyme of poetry to engage young readers. Poetry helps develop language skills and is often used in phonemic awareness techniques. Moreover, since poetry often uses figurative speech, it encourages imagination and creative thinking. As students progress, their enjoyment of poetry grows to encompass different forms and styles. Most students not only enjoy reading poetry, but they enjoy creating their own verse as well. Finally, most assessment tests now include poetry. These tests include both multiple choice and short-answer questions. It is important that students become comfortable with the format so as to be confident when they encounter it in testing situations.

The Poetry Series

This reproducible poetry series will supplement any reading program. Each lesson tests comprehension skills as well as offers suggestions for vocabulary and fluency development, two essential skills for reading and language development.

Organization of the Poetry Series

The book is divided into four thematic units which will help the teacher integrate poetry into other content areas. The units are A Variety of Verse, Reflections in Rhyme, Poems of People, and Tales to Tell. There are five poems in each unit. The lesson components are explained below.

Teacher Information

The first page of every lesson provides explicit instructions for teaching the poem. There are specific sections that address multiple skills. To begin, each poem is summarized. A list of words that students may find difficult to read or understand is included as well. Another section lists a specific poetry standard and outlines an activity that will help students explore the concept. A third section outlines how to introduce the poem and the vocabulary words, as well as includes ideas for fluency practice. Finally, a fun and creative writing suggestion helps children think about the topic or a specific skill to extend the lesson.

Poem

The poems were selected to complement topics taught at each grade level. Illustrations on the page support the topic to help children better understand the content.

Assessment

Each poem is followed by a seven-question assessment. The first six questions are in a standardized-test format and focus on six important comprehension skills. They always follow a prescribed order:

1. Facts The first question focuses on literal comprehension. Students identify pieces of factual information. They look for details that tell who, what, when, where, and how.

2. Sequence The second question refers to sequence. Students practice identifying the order of events or the steps in a process.

3. Context In the third question, students are required to practice using all the words in the poem to understand unfamiliar words. Students become aware of the relationships between words, phrases, and sentences.

4. Main Idea In this question, students will identify the overall point made in the poem. Students must be able to differentiate between the main idea and details.

5. Conclusion The fifth question requires students to draw conclusions. Conclusions are not stated in the reading but must be formulated. Students draw conclusions based only on the information in the poem.

6. Inference The sixth question asks students to make inferences by combining their own knowledge and experience with what they read. They put the facts together to make a reasonable inference about something that is not stated in the poem.

7. Short Answer The final question requires that children write a brief response to a higher-level question.

Other Components

• **Standards** A list of grade-level, poetry-specific standards is found on page 5. A chart highlights in which lesson each standard is introduced.

• **Glossary** Poetry terms and definitions for use by the teacher and older students are given on page 6. Some of the elements are not introduced to younger students in this poetry series since they require advanced knowledge.

• **General Assessment** A two-page assessment is found on pages 7 and 8. It can be used as a pretest to gauge students' understanding of the comprehension skills. It can also be used as a posttest to determine improvements after exposure to poetic literature.

• **Graphic Organizers** Five graphic organizers are provided on pages 9–13 to support different activities and skill development suggested in various lessons.

Poetry: Grade 5, SV 9895-7

Poetry Standards • Grade 5

The following standards focus specifically on poetry and are accepted by many states as important to students in the fifth grade.

Standard	Lesson
Distinguish between fiction, nonfiction, poetry, and plays	1
Identify rhyme	9, 11
Identify rhythm	7
Recognize the use of repetition in poetry	5
Identify a haiku poem	2
Identify a free verse poem	3, 6
Identify a diamante	4
Identify a ballad	17
Identify the use of figurative language (simile, metaphor, personification, dialect)	8, 10, 12, 13, 14, 15, 20
Identify elements of story structure in fiction and poetry (characterization, setting, events of the plot, and solution)	16, 18, 19 specifically; All poems
Read stories, poems, and passages with fluency, utilizing appropriate rhythm, pacing, intonation, and expression	All poems

Resources: Standards
Poetry: Grade 5, SV 9895-7

Glossary

alliteration the repetition of the same beginning sound, usually a consonant, in a phrase or line of poetry. Tongue twisters use alliteration. Example: *She sells seashells by the seashore.*

analogy a likeness between two things that are not alike in other ways. Example: *the wings of a bird and the arms of a person*

assonance the repetition of similar vowel sounds in words so they are close in sound but do not rhyme. Example: *She feeds the deer.*

ballad a long poem written about a famous person or event

cinquain a formula poem that has five lines and a total of 22 syllables, distributed in a specific 2–4–6–8–2 pattern

concrete a poem in which the words, letters, or shape of the poem matches the topic

consonance the close repetition of identical consonant sounds before and after different vowels. Example: *flip—flop; feel—fill*

diamante a formula poem that is shaped like a diamond, and the words describe opposite ideas

haiku a formula poem that has three lines and a total of 17 syllables, often distributed in a specific 5–7–5 pattern

imagery the author's use of description and words to create pictures in the reader's mind

limerick a humorous formula poem that has five lines, an "aabba" rhyming pattern, and a specific rhythm

metaphor the comparison of two things in which one is said to be another. Metaphors do not use the words *like* or *as*. Example: *The lake was a golden mirror.*

meter the cadence, or beat, of a poem

onomatopoeia a sound device in which a word makes the sound. Examples: *crash, bang*

personification a device in which human qualities and ideas are given to things. Example: *The wind whispered through the trees.*

poetry an expression of ideas or feeling in words. Poetry usually has form, rhythm, and rhyme.

repetition a sound device in which sounds, words, or phrases are repeated to emphasize a point

rhyme two or more lines that end with rhyming words

rhyming words words that end in the same sounds

rhythm the repeated meter, or beat, in a poem

simile the comparison of two things that are not really alike by using the words *like* or *as*. Example: *Her smile was like sunshine.*

sonnet a poem with 14 lines and a specific rhyming and rhythm pattern

stanza a group of related lines in a poem

tanka a formula poem that has five lines and a total of 31 syllables, distributed in a specific 5–7–5–7–7 pattern

To Any Reader
by Robert Louis Stevenson

As from the house your mother sees
You playing round the garden trees,
So you may see, if you will look
Through the windows of this book,
Another child, far, far away,
And in another garden, play.
But do not think you can at all,
By knocking on the window, call
That child to hear you. He intent
Is all on his play-business bent.
He does not hear, he will not look,
Nor yet be lured out of this book.
For, long ago, the truth to say,
He has grown up and gone away,
And it is but a child of air
That lingers in the garden there.

Go on to the next page.

Assessment
Poetry: Grade 5, SV 9895-7

To Any Reader: Assessment

Think about the poem. Then answer the questions. Fill in the circle next to the correct answer.

1. What is the child in the poem doing?
   Ⓐ reading a book
   Ⓑ playing in a garden
   Ⓒ playing with friends
   Ⓓ playing with a pet

2. Since the time the other child was in the garden, he has
   Ⓐ grown and gone away.
   Ⓑ gone inside the house.
   Ⓒ climbed into the tree.
   Ⓓ disappeared.

3. The child is "intent" on his play. This probably means that
   Ⓐ he is tired of the game.
   Ⓑ he is not paying attention to what he is doing.
   Ⓒ he is playing in a tent.
   Ⓓ he is concentrating on playing.

4. This poem is mostly about
   Ⓐ a boy in a poetry book.
   Ⓑ what happens to little boys.
   Ⓒ playing in a garden.
   Ⓓ how children are alike.

5. The boy cannot be called because
   Ⓐ he is not able to hear.
   Ⓑ the garden is too noisy.
   Ⓒ he refuses to listen.
   Ⓓ he is an imaginary child.

6. Although the poem is called "To Any Reader," the poet appears to expect that
   Ⓐ people will think that the child in the poem is real.
   Ⓑ his poems will not be appreciated.
   Ⓒ children will be reading the book.
   Ⓓ his book will never be read.

7. What happens when the boy in the poetry book tries to call the child in the garden?

   _____

   _____

   _____

Poetry: Grade 5, SV 9895-7

KWHL Chart

L (What did I LEARN?)	H (HOW will I learn?)	W (What do I WANT to know?)	K (What do I KNOW?)

Resources: KWHL Chart
Poetry: Grade 5, SV 9895-7

Word Web

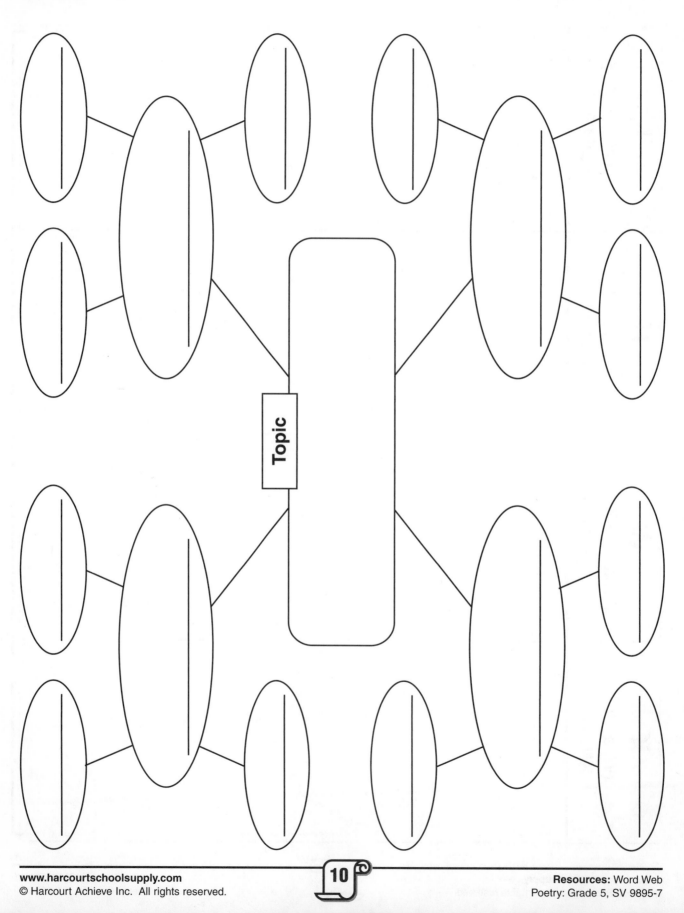

Topic

Resources: Word Web
Poetry: Grade 5, SV 9895-7

Word Card

What Is the Word?
Write the word here.

_____

What Does the Word Mean?
Write the meaning here.

_____

_____

_____

_____

_____

_____

_____

_____

What Does the Word Stand For?
Draw a picture of it here.

How Can You Use the Word?
Write a sentence using the word here.

_____

_____

_____

_____

_____

_____

_____

_____

Resources: Word Card
Poetry: Grade 5, SV 9895-7

Name _____   Date _____

Venn Diagram

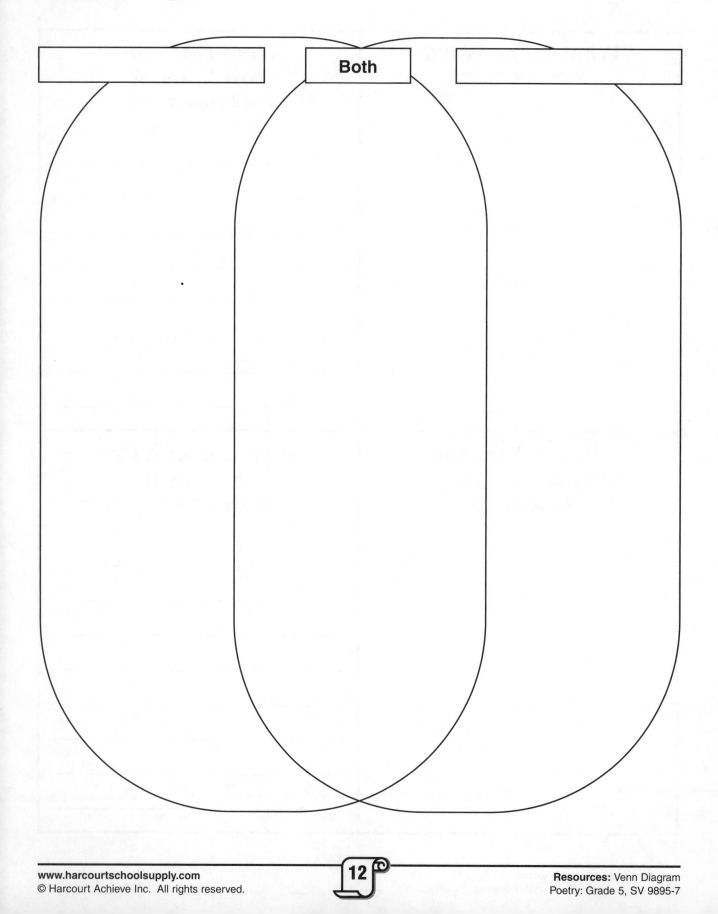

Both

Resources: Venn Diagram
Poetry: Grade 5, SV 9895-7

Name _____   Date _____

Story Map

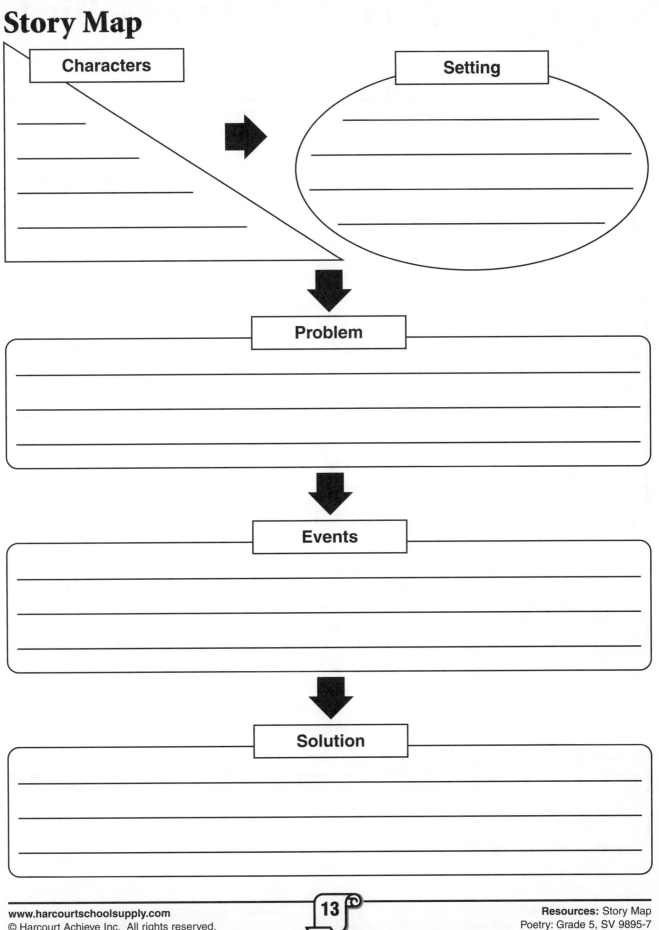

Characters

Setting

Problem

Events

Solution

Resources: Story Map
Poetry: Grade 5, SV 9895-7

[from] The Dinkey-Bird

Poetry Skill: Format

Standard
Distinguish between fiction, nonfiction, poetry, and plays

Explore the Format of a Poem
Display a story and lead students in a discussion of the format, including paragraph formation and sentence length. Then pass out the poem. Have the students compare and contrast the poem and the story formats. Point out poem terms, including *lines* and *stanzas,* as the students identify them. Guide students to understand that many poems have short lines and that lack of punctuation at the end of line breaks signals that the sentence continues on the next line.

Vocabulary

ardor–a feeling of strong eagerness
damper–restraint or discouragement
naught–nothing
romping–leaping and frisking about in play
sapient–wise
scamper–to run or go quickly and lightly
whither–to what or which place

Summary

The poem describes an imaginary land for children to visit, a place where candy grows on trees, birds are always singing, and the children can play all day.

Read the Poem

Introduce the Poem
Lead students in a discussion of what it would be like to live on an island that was only available to young people. Tell students that they will read a poem about such a place.

Introduce the Vocabulary
Write several sets of vocabulary words on index cards. Pass them out so that each student has a word. Write each word on the board, say it, and give its definition. Ask students holding that card to form a group. After all words have been named, ask each group to write a sentence using the word. Have students share sentences.

After Reading

Questions
1. Where is the land of Wonder-Wander? (*in an ocean, far away*)
2. Why do children love to go to Wonder-Wander? (*Possible response: because candy grows like plants and children are allowed to play as loudly and wildly as they choose.*)
3. What is another good title for this poem? (*Answers will vary.*)

Fluency
Remind students that one sentence may be written on several lines in a poem, making it difficult to know how to read the text. Point out that the punctuation at the end of the line can help them decide how to read the sentence. Then read the first verse, modeling how to pause or continue reading smoothly for the different punctuation marks. Then invite partners to practice reading the first stanza of the poem.

Develop Oral Language
Have each student record the poem on a tape recorder and discuss the level of fluency that was demonstrated with a partner.

Writing

Have students think of their own imaginary land and invite them to write a poem describing it.

[from] The Dinkey-Bird

by Eugene Field

In an ocean, 'way out yonder,
(As all sapient people know)
Is the land of Wonder-Wander,
Whither children love to go;
It's their playing, romping, swinging,
That give great joy to me
While the Dinkey-Bird goes singing
In the amfalula tree!

There the gum-drops grow like cherries,
And taffy's thick as peas—
Caramels you pick like berries
When, and where, and how you please;
Big red sugar-plums are clinging
To the cliffs beside that sea
Where the Dinkey-Bird is singing
In the amfalula tree!

So when children shout and scamper
And make merry all the day,
When there's naught to put a damper
To the ardor of their play;
When I hear their laughter ringing,
Then I'm sure as sure can be
That the Dinkey-Bird is singing
In the amfalula tree!

Name _____   Date _____

[from] The Dinkey-Bird: Assessment

Think about the poem. Then answer the questions. Fill in the circle next to the correct answer.

1. What kind of food grows in the land of Wonder-Wander?
   - Ⓐ candy
   - Ⓑ fruits
   - Ⓒ seafood
   - Ⓓ vegetables

2. When is the poet sure that the Dinkey-Bird is singing?
   - Ⓐ when he sees the bird in the tree
   - Ⓑ when it is morning
   - Ⓒ when he hears the children laughing
   - Ⓓ before the children arrive

3. "Sapient" most likely means
   - Ⓐ silly.
   - Ⓑ wise.
   - Ⓒ strange.
   - Ⓓ quiet.

4. This poem is mainly about
   - Ⓐ how foolish children can be.
   - Ⓑ a place where children are sent.
   - Ⓒ an island full of strange birds.
   - Ⓓ a fun place for children to visit.

5. It seems to be the poet's opinion that
   - Ⓐ a child's favorite kind of bird is a Dinkey-Bird.
   - Ⓑ children would enjoy a place where candy grows.
   - Ⓒ children should go far away across the ocean.
   - Ⓓ children should be quiet.

6. Which of these probably describes the poet's feelings for children?
   - Ⓐ He is fond of them.
   - Ⓑ He does not have the patience for them.
   - Ⓒ He is not comfortable around them.
   - Ⓓ He thinks they should act like adults.

7. What clues tell you that this poem is about an imaginary land?

   _____

   _____

   _____

Name _____   Date _____

Word Puzzle

Use the clues and the words in the box to complete the crossword puzzle.

damper	romping	naught	sapient	scamper	whither

Across
2. to run or go quickly and lightly
4. restraint or discouragement
5. to what or which place

Down
1. nothing
2. wise
3. leaping and frisking about in play

Nature's Haikus

**Poetry Skill:
Haiku Poetry**

Standard
Identify a haiku poem

Explore Haiku Poetry
A haiku contains 17 syllables, divided into three unrhymed lines of 5, 7, and 5 syllables. It captures a single vivid image of nature in a single moment. Write the first line of the first haiku on the board and draw lines to divide the syllables: Pond/wa/ter/rip/pling. Have a student count the number of syllables and write it at the end of the line. Continue with this process for the remainder of the first haiku. Point out the formula as you go along.

Vocabulary

anxiously–with painful uncertainty
breaks–forces or makes way through; penetrates
depth–a deep part or place
quenching–satisfying
renewing–making new again
rippling–forming small waves

Summary

Three haiku poems focus on forms of water.

Read the Poem

Introduce the Poem
Remind students that often a haiku is an observation about nature. Lead the students in discussing that all three of the haikus reflect observation of water in its natural forms.

Introduce the Vocabulary
Ask the students to work in small groups and choose one word from the haikus that they would like to know more about. Then have groups research their word. They may need the assistance of a dictionary. Ask each group to write the definition of the word and a sentence using the word on the board. Discuss each group's response.

After Reading

Questions
1. What tells you that each poem is a haiku? (*the formula for a haiku: 5–7–5 syllable pattern*)
2. What is the setting for each of the three haikus? (*Haiku 1: a natural pond, Haiku 2: a rain forest or anywhere that it's raining, Haiku 3: the beach*)
3. Is the poet's mood the same in all three haikus? If not, look at each haiku and decide the mood the poet is in. (*No, the mood is not the same. In Haikus 1 and 2, the mood is quiet and reflective. In Haiku 3, the mood is one of excitement and anticipation.*)

Fluency
Point out to students that although haikus are alike in that they are observations of nature, each one can have a different mood or feeling. This can affect the way it is read aloud. Have students notice that the third haiku has an exclamation point at the end. This signals that it should be read with excitement.

Develop Oral Language
Have students work with a partner to practice reading the poems fluently and with expression. Once they feel comfortable reading the poems, encourage volunteers to read a haiku in front of the class.

Writing

Have students think of a scene in nature and use the word web on page 10 to organize the sights, sounds, colors, and actions that they associate with it. Have students use these words as imagery in their haiku.

Name _____   Date _____

Nature's Haikus

Haiku 1
Pond water rippling,
the stone breaks into its depth,
falling on soft sand.

Haiku 2
Softly misting rain,
quenching the bright flowers' thirst,
renewing their life.

Haiku 3
Anxiously waiting,
waves crashing against the shore,
treasures left behind!

Understand the Poem

Nature's Haikus: Assessment

 ✎— **Think about the poem. Then answer the questions. Fill in the circle next to the correct answer.**

1. In the first haiku, what fell on soft sand?
   - Ⓐ pond water
   - Ⓑ flowers
   - Ⓒ a stone
   - Ⓓ the waves

2. In the second haiku, what happens after the rain quenches the flowers' thirst?
   - Ⓐ The rain drowns the flowers.
   - Ⓑ The rain stops.
   - Ⓒ The sun comes out.
   - Ⓓ The rain renews their life.

3. The word "quenching" in the second haiku most likely means
   - Ⓐ satisfying.
   - Ⓑ thirst.
   - Ⓒ drying.
   - Ⓓ growing.

4. A good title for the third haiku would be
   - Ⓐ "Catch a Wave."
   - Ⓑ "Seashells."
   - Ⓒ "Anticipation."
   - Ⓓ "Pirate's Bounty."

5. From these three haikus you can conclude that
   - Ⓐ water makes plants grow.
   - Ⓑ water can be measured.
   - Ⓒ water can take different forms.
   - Ⓓ water moves in a variety of ways.

6. It would seem that the poet
   - Ⓐ walks along the beach.
   - Ⓑ makes observations about nature.
   - Ⓒ enjoys swimming.
   - Ⓓ None of the above

7. How does the poet's mood change in each haiku?

_____

_____

_____

_____

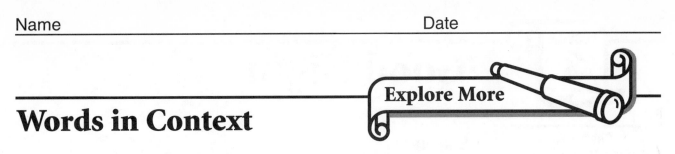

Words in Context

Explore More

Use other words in sentences to help you find the missing word.

➤ Read the story. Think about the meanings of the words in bold type.

Fishing Day

The still water becomes rough as it goes **rippling** over the rocks at the fishing hole. Aaron's lure **breaks** the surface of the water as he casts. Large catfish swim in the dark **depth** of the pond. Aaron sits in the shade of a large elm tree, **quenching** his thirst with an ice-cold lemonade from the cooler. Suddenly, after hours of **anxiously** waiting, Aaron jumps to his feet! A catfish nibbles on the bait, **renewing** Aaron's hopes of catching big Granddaddy catfish!

➤ Look at the words in bold type. Use clues in the story to figure out the meaning of each word. Write each word on the line next to its meaning.

_____ **1.** making new again

_____ **2.** satisfying

_____ **3.** a deep part or place

_____ **4.** forming small waves

_____ **5.** forces or makes way through

_____ **6.** with painful uncertainty

Lesson 2 • Nature's Haikus: Vocabulary Skill
Poetry: Grade 5, SV 9895-7

LESSON 3

Good Night

Poetry Skill: Free Verse Poetry

Standard
Identify a free verse poem

Explore Free Verse Poetry
Explain to students that this poem is an example of free verse poetry. This is a style of poetry with no set length or rhyme scheme. Free verse poetry seems to break all the rules. The writer decides how the poem should look, feel, and sound.

Vocabulary

baritone–a sound that is lower in range than a tenor and higher than bass
lowland–an area of land that is low and flat
mushrooming–spreading or developing quickly
pillar–an upright structure such as a column
razorback–a sharp ridged hill
smokestack–a pipe for smoke or gases to escape
spell–to signify or mean
trajectory–the path followed by a moving object

Research Base

"To appreciate poetry is to appreciate the art of language." *(Guiding Readers and Writers: Grades 3–6, p. 410)*

Summary

Using free verse, Carl Sandburg gives examples of ways to "spell" or signify that it is night.

Read the Poem

Introduce the Poem
Use the word web on page 10 (as an overhead transparency) to brainstorm information about *night*. Guide students to understand that each person has ideas that establish images of night. Tell students that this poem contains Carl Sandburg's thoughts about things that make a night "good."

Introduce the Vocabulary
Write the vocabulary words and the definitions on the board. Lead students in a brief discussion of the words. Then have students create a crossword puzzle with the vocabulary words using graph paper. Challenge students to write sentences for the clues.

After Reading

Activity
Write the words *good night* in the middle circle of the word web from page 10. Ask students to give examples of the imagery Carl Sandburg used in order to "spell good night." Complete the word web with their responses. This word web may be used later as a model when students write their own free verse poem.

Fluency
Explain that free verse poetry can seem difficult to read because it lacks a rhythm or beat that is easy to hear. The poet simply wrote down his or her thoughts and used imagery. Explain that it is important to pay attention to the punctuation; however, the tone of the reader's voice and the pace at which the poem is read will create the mental image for the listener. Model reading the poem for the students.

Develop Oral Language
Have students take turns reading the poem to one another. Remind them that the content of the poem often gives a clue as to how to read it. Challenge the students to read the poem the way the poet would read it.

Writing

Have students brainstorm topics for a free verse poem. Encourage students to use the word web on page 10 to organize their thoughts. After students complete the web, have them write a free verse poem and illustrate it.

Good Night
by Carl Sandburg

MANY ways to spell good night.

Fireworks at a pier on the Fourth of July
spell it with red wheels and yellow spokes.
They fizz in the air, touch the water and quit.
Rockets make a trajectory of gold-and-blue
and then go out.

Railroad trains at night
spell with a smokestack mushrooming a white pillar.

Steamboats turn a curve in the Mississippi
crying in a baritone
that crosses lowland cottonfields to a razorback hill.

It is easy to spell good night.
Many ways to spell good night.

Name _____   Date _____

Good Night: Assessment

✒ **Think about the poem. Then answer the questions. Fill in the circle next to the correct answer.**

1. What "spells good night" with a variety of colors?
   Ⓐ railroad trains at night
   Ⓑ steamboats
   Ⓒ crying
   Ⓓ fireworks at a pier

2. What happens to the fireworks after they "fizz in the air"?
   Ⓐ They turn into rockets.
   Ⓑ They produce the colors blue and gold.
   Ⓒ They fall into the water.
   Ⓓ They "spell good night" with red wheels and yellow spokes.

3. The poet uses the phrase "many ways to spell good night." In this phrase, the word "spell" means
   Ⓐ to signify.
   Ⓑ to write.
   Ⓒ a fit.
   Ⓓ a length of time.

4. The poem is mostly about
   Ⓐ colors of fireworks.
   Ⓑ forms of transportation.
   Ⓒ images of night.
   Ⓓ sounds of steamboats.

5. The season of this poem is
   Ⓐ winter.
   Ⓑ spring.
   Ⓒ summer.
   Ⓓ fall.

6. Which of these seems true of the poet?
   Ⓐ He is annoyed by the sights and sounds of summer.
   Ⓑ He has fond memories of summer nights.
   Ⓒ He prefers to spend time outside during the day.
   Ⓓ None of the above

7. What are some other ways the poet might "spell good night"?

   _____

   _____

   _____

Compound Words

A compound word is a word made by putting two or more words together.
   Example: door + bell = doorbell

Draw a line to make a compound word. Match one word from the first column with one from the second column. Use each word only once. Write each new word in a box. Then, draw a picture to show its meaning.

1. smoke   fields

2. steam   stack

3. cotton   land

4. low   boat

    _____	 _____
    _____	 _____

Opposites

Standard
Identify a diamante

Explore a Diamante
A *diamante* is a 7-line diamond-shaped poem that contrasts opposite noun pairs. The first half of the poem describes the first noun in the pair while the second half of the poem describes the other noun. The formula for a diamante is **Line 1:** 1 noun; **Line 2:** 2 adjectives that describe line 1; **Line 3:** 3 verbs that end in *-ing* and describe line 1; **Line 4:** 4 nouns, first 2 refer to line 1 and the next 2 nouns refer to line 7; **Line 5:** 3 verbs that end in *-ing* and describe line 7; **Line 6:** 2 adjectives that describe line 7; **Line 7:** 1 noun that is the opposite of line 1.

Vocabulary

descending–coming down
disguising–changing the appearance of
emerging–coming into view
radiant–emitting heat or light
revealing–showing
subsiding–sinking
temperate–mild

Summary

Two diamante poems show how poets can create an image in the reader's mind simply by contrasting two opposite nouns.

Read the Poem

Introduce the Poem
Have students look at the poems. Ask them what is different about these poems from other poems that they have read. Tell the students that each of the poems is shaped like a diamond, and they are called diamante poems. Explain the shape of the poems is not as important as how the words are arranged. Share with students the formula that a diamante poem must follow.

Introduce the Vocabulary
Write the vocabulary words and the definitions on separate cards. Put them in a pocket chart in any order. Say a sentence with a vocabulary word and ask a volunteer to find the word and its definition. Then, have students name a word that is the opposite of that vocabulary word. Write the opposite word on a card and place it next to the vocabulary word.

After Reading

Activity
Provide each student with two copies of the word web on page 10 to write the pair of opposite nouns from the poems along with their verbs and adjectives. This activity will enable the students to see each topic as separate and less confusing.

Fluency
Help students explore how to read poems with commas. Remind them that a comma signals a pause. Then have students practice reading the poem fluently.

Develop Oral Language
Have partners alternate reading the poem.

Writing

Have students write a "Diamante for Two." Have each student write the first half of a diamante, stopping on the fourth line after the second noun. Then have students switch papers with a partner. Challenge students to write the final half of the diamante they have been given. Have students return original diamantes to one another. Encourage students to discuss their completed poems. Have them illustrate their poems and display them.

Name _____   Date _____

Opposites
by Anonymous

Sunrise
beautiful, joyful
emerging, shining, rising
dawn, morning, dusk, evening
fading, subsiding, descending
remarkable, peaceful
Sunset

Day
radiant, tropical
steaming, shining, revealing
daybreak, noon, nightfall, midnight
cooling, shading, disguising
moonlit, temperate
Night

Name _____   Date _____

Opposites: Assessment

➤ **Think about the poem. Then answer the questions. Fill in the circle next to the correct answer.**

1. In the first diamante, what does the poet contrast the sunrise to?
   Ⓐ dawn
   Ⓑ sunset
   Ⓒ day
   Ⓓ night

2. What time of day occurs most closely before midnight?
   Ⓐ daybreak
   Ⓑ morning
   Ⓒ noon
   Ⓓ nightfall

3. In the first diamante, the sun is "emerging" at sunrise. "Emerging" means
   Ⓐ rising.
   Ⓑ disguising.
   Ⓒ declining.
   Ⓓ fading.

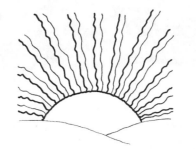

4. What was the poet's purpose in writing these diamantes?
   Ⓐ to relate feelings about the times that occur during a day
   Ⓑ to describe a favorite time of day
   Ⓒ to compare opposite times of day
   Ⓓ to explain the times that occur during a day

5. The reader can conclude that both diamantes
   Ⓐ take place over a period of one week.
   Ⓑ take place in a twenty-four hour period.
   Ⓒ take place over a period of one month.
   Ⓓ None of the above

6. The poet is probably
   Ⓐ a person who sees the negative side of things.
   Ⓑ a person who shows no emotion.
   Ⓒ a person who needs cheering up.
   Ⓓ a person who sees the positive side of things.

7. What is the purpose of writing a diamante?

_____

_____

_____

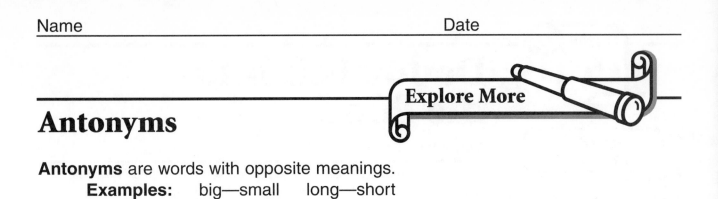

Explore More

Antonyms

Antonyms are words with opposite meanings.
    Examples: big—small   long—short

Find a word in the second column that means the opposite of the word in the first column. Write the letter of the antonym from the second column on the line beside each word.

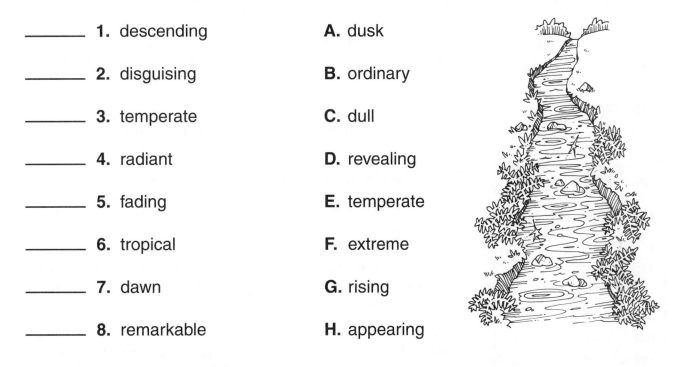

_____ **1.** descending   **A.** dusk

_____ **2.** disguising   **B.** ordinary

_____ **3.** temperate   **C.** dull

_____ **4.** radiant   **D.** revealing

_____ **5.** fading   **E.** temperate

_____ **6.** tropical   **F.** extreme

_____ **7.** dawn   **G.** rising

_____ **8.** remarkable   **H.** appearing

Use each word from the box to write a sentence.

descending	remarkable	fading	radiant	tropical

9. _____

_____

_____

_____

_____

Lesson 4 • Opposites: Vocabulary Skill
Poetry: Grade 5, SV 9895-7

LESSON 5

Daddy Fell into the Pond

Vocabulary

beyond–in addition to
daft–crazy or insane
dismal–dark and gloomy; cheerless
drake–a male duck
duckweed–a plant that floats on water and forms thick green scum on top of the water
respond–to react

Teacher Tips

Make the introduction of this lesson more interesting by using photos from your own childhood! Share photos from a memorable event that took place when you were young. This will encourage your students to begin thinking of "everyday" events and how these events can become a story or a poem.

Summary

The poet remembers a "dismal" day from his youth that quickly became quite bright due to his father's falling unexpectedly into the pond.

Read the Poem

Introduce the Poem
Ask students to share humorous or memorable family experiences. Tell students that they will read a poem about a child whose "dismal" day turned memorable because of an accident.

Introduce the Vocabulary
Have students work in small groups. Assign a vocabulary word and provide a dictionary for each group. First, ask the groups to guess what their word means. Then, have students use the dictionary to find the definition of the word. Have each group write a sentence using the word. Finally, have each group present its guess, the correct definition, and the sentence to the class.

After Reading

Activity
Remind the students that poems have a sequence. Make a sequence of events story board with your students. Give each student a 6" x 9" piece of white construction paper. Have the students fold the paper in half twice. Now the students have four sections on the paper. As you review the sequence of the events in the poem, have students illustrate an event in each section. For a more advanced story board, encourage the students to make additional folds.

Fluency
Remind students that one sentence may be written on several lines in a poem, making it hard to know how to read the text. Point out that the punctuation at the end of the line can help them decide how to read the sentence. Then read the first verse of the poem, modeling how to pause or continue reading smoothly for the different punctuation marks.

Develop Oral Language
Have partners reread the poem and alternate reading the verses. Challenge them to read the poem fluently, using the punctuation marks as clues.

Writing

Have the students prepare a story board about a funny family accident or event. Then invite them to write a paragraph describing the situation. Remind students to include details of the event and how other people reacted to what happened. Challenge students to turn their paragraph into a poem.

Daddy Fell into the Pond

by Alfred Noyes

Everyone grumbled. The sky was grey.
We had nothing to do and nothing to say.
We were nearing the end of a dismal day,
And then there seemed to be nothing beyond,
Then
Daddy fell into the pond!

And everyone's face grew merry and bright,
And Timothy danced for sheer delight.
"Give me the camera, quick, oh quick!
He's crawling out of the duckweed!" Click!

Then the gardener suddenly slapped his knee,
And doubled up, shaking silently,
And the ducks all quacked as if they were daft,
And it sounded as if the old drake laughed.
Oh, there wasn't a thing that didn't respond
When
Daddy fell into the pond!

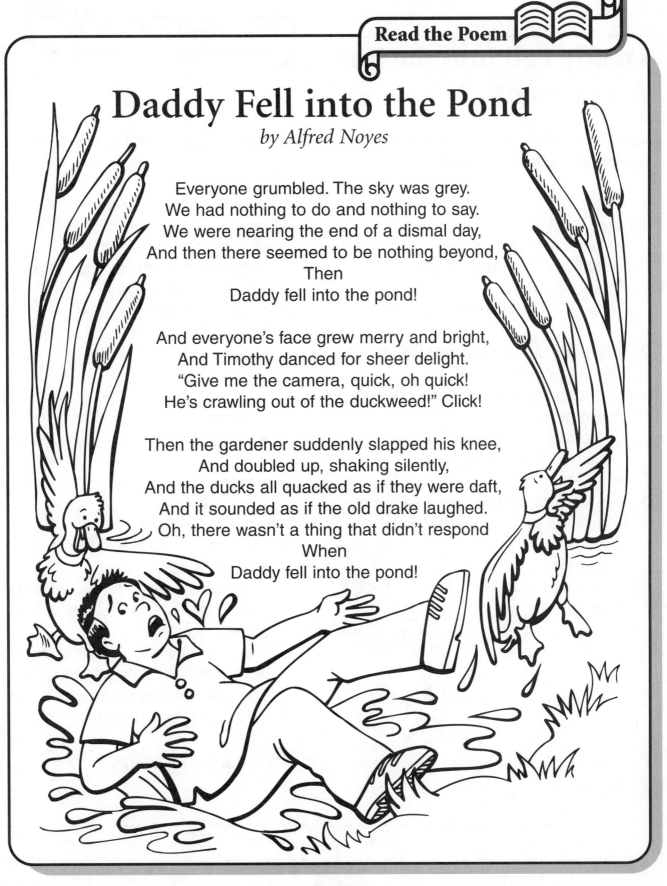

Daddy Fell into the Pond: Assessment

Think about the poem. Then answer the questions. Fill in the circle next to the correct answer.

1. The gardener "suddenly slapped his knee" and
   Ⓐ grabbed the camera.
   Ⓑ danced for sheer delight.
   Ⓒ shook silently.
   Ⓓ helped Daddy out of the pond.

2. What did Timothy do after Daddy fell into the pond?
   Ⓐ He crawled out of the duckweed.
   Ⓑ He grumbled.
   Ⓒ He took a picture of Daddy.
   Ⓓ He didn't respond at all.

3. The poet says, "We were nearing the end of a dismal day." What does "dismal" mean?
   Ⓐ gloomy
   Ⓑ exciting
   Ⓒ grey
   Ⓓ brief

4. The poet's purpose in writing this poem was
   Ⓐ to make fun of his father.
   Ⓑ to describe an experience that was very memorable.
   Ⓒ to describe his childhood.
   Ⓓ to explain how to take a photograph.

5. What is the setting of this poem?
   Ⓐ a city park
   Ⓑ a forest stream
   Ⓒ a pond
   Ⓓ a lake

6. Which is most likely true?
   Ⓐ The poet would like to forget about this day.
   Ⓑ The poet's uneventful day turned into an interesting day due to his father's accident.
   Ⓒ The poet didn't really notice that his father had fallen into the pond.
   Ⓓ The poet wanted his day to continue to be uneventful.

7. What did the poet mean when he wrote, "Oh, there wasn't a thing that didn't respond"?

_____

_____

Words in Context

Use other words in sentences to help you find the missing word.

Read each sentence. Find a word from the box to complete it. Then write the word on the line.

merry	respond	complained	quickly	daft	dismal

1. We all felt it was a _____ day and that nothing exciting was going to happen.

2. Everyone _____ because they were upset that nothing interesting seemed to be happening.

3. The mood suddenly turned _____ as we laughed when Daddy fell into the pond.

4. We watched the gardener suddenly _____ by slapping his knee and silently shaking.

5. Timothy _____ grabbed the camera to take a picture of the sudden event.

6. The ducks began to quack madly, as if they were

   _____, when Daddy fell into the pond.

Geography

Summary

In this free verse poem, the poet explains how she understands the geography of her surroundings. She has observed the different trees that grow in different areas, and this has helped her understand her world.

Read the Poem

Introduce the Poem

Use a book about trees (see Teacher Tips) to introduce the concept of geography. Discuss the geography of your area. Have students give examples of trees or other plants that grow in your area. Tell students that they will be reading a free verse poem that the poet wrote about the observations she has made about trees and where they grow.

Introduce the Vocabulary

Write the vocabulary words on the board. Discuss the definition of each word.

After Reading

Questions

1. What kind of words does the poet use to describe the trees in the poem? (*adjectives*)
2. What type of figurative language does the poet use to compare the trees to other things around her? (*She uses similes.*)

Fluency

Explain that free verse poetry can seem difficult to read because it lacks a rhythm or beat that is easy to hear. The poet simply wrote down her thoughts. She used adjectives and comparisons to make the poem interesting. Explain that it is important to pay attention to the punctuation that is used. The tone of the reader's voice and the pace at which the poem is read will create the mental image for the listener. Model reading the poem for the students.

Develop Oral Language

Have students work with a partner to practice reading the poem. Point out to the students that this poem has line breaks that do not have end punctuation. Remind them to read the sentence smoothly and fluently when there is no end punctuation.

Writing

Have students write a free verse poem about something that is part of their geography. Have them write their thoughts without concern for meter or rhyme. Encourage them to use adjectives and comparisons to give readers a clear mental picture of their thoughts.

Name _____ Date _____

Geography
by Hilda Conkling

I can tell balsam trees
By their grayish bluish silverish look of smoke.
Pine trees fringe out.
Hemlocks look like Christmas.
The spruce tree is feathered and rough
Like the legs of the red chickens in our poultry yard.
I can study my geography from chickens
Named for Plymouth Rock and Rhode Island,
And from trees out of Canada.
No; I shall leave the chickens out.
I shall make a new geography of my own.
I shall have a hillside of spruce and hemlock
Like a separate country,
And I shall mark a walk of spires on my map,
A secret road of balsam trees
With blue buds.
Trees that smell like a wind out of fairy-land
Where little people live
Who need no geography
But trees.

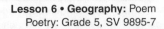

Geography: Assessment

➤ **Think about the poem. Then answer the questions. Fill in the circle next to the correct answer.**

1. Who are the "little people" in the poem?
   - Ⓐ chickens
   - Ⓑ trees
   - Ⓒ fairies
   - Ⓓ the poet's friends

2. After she talks about the chickens, the poet
   - Ⓐ decides to leave them out.
   - Ⓑ forgets about them.
   - Ⓒ realizes that they are like trees.
   - Ⓓ thinks about dinner.

3. "Poultry" probably means the same as
   - Ⓐ back.
   - Ⓑ fowl.
   - Ⓒ tree.
   - Ⓓ farm.

4. The main idea of this poem is
   - Ⓐ that chickens are like trees.
   - Ⓑ that different types of trees grow in different places.
   - Ⓒ that the poet does not care for geography.
   - Ⓓ that geography is like a fairy tale.

5. You can conclude that the poet
   - Ⓐ has studied the trees around her.
   - Ⓑ knows nothing about chickens.
   - Ⓒ is a poor geography student.
   - Ⓓ lives in a fairy-land.

6. It is likely that the poet
   - Ⓐ has no schoolbooks to study from.
   - Ⓑ lives in a densely populated area.
   - Ⓒ spends much of her time with nature.
   - Ⓓ None of the above

7. How do you know that this is a free verse poem?

_____

_____

_____

_____

Name _____   Date _____

Make a Picture

How do you picture words? Sometimes the picture you draw in your mind can help you remember the meanings of words.
Example: forest

Draw a picture for each of the vocabulary words below. Then, use each word in a sentence showing you understand what it means.

1. feathered	**2.** spires
3. poultry	**4.** fringe

Escape at Bedtime

**Poetry Skill:
Rhythm**

Standard
Identify rhythm

Explore Meter
Explain to students that many poems have a specific rhythm, or beat. The beat is called meter. Meter is a pattern. Tell students that some poets follow the same pattern, while others vary the pattern from verse to verse. Write the first line of the poem on the board and draw lines to divide the syllables. (The/lights/from/ the/par/lor/and/kitch/en/ shone/out.) Then, write the number of syllables at the end of the line. (11) Then have partners find the number of syllables for the remaining lines to find the poem's meter. Discuss the pattern that the poet used in this poem.

Vocabulary

glittered–shone with bright, sparkling lights
glory–radiant beauty; magnificence; splendor
overhead–above one's head
packed–pressed or crowded together
parlor–a room in a home for receiving visitors

Summary

Robert Louis Stevenson paints the scene of a young child enjoying star gazing. As the child goes to bed, the memory of the stars remains with him.

Read the Poem

Introduce the Poem

Introduce the word *constellation* to the students. Lead the students in a discussion about constellations by utilizing the KWHL chart from page 9 as a transparency on the overhead projector to record what students know about constellations.

Introduce the Vocabulary

Write the vocabulary words on the board. Have the students work in small groups to brainstorm a definition for each word.

After Reading

Questions

1. How many stars did the poet see? (*thousands of millions*)
2. What two things does Robert Louis Stevenson compare to the number of stars in the sky? (*the leaves on the trees, the people in church or in the park*)
3. Why do you think the poet uses comparisons in this poem? (*Possible response: to create a picture of just how many stars there are for the reader*)

Fluency

Remind students that sometimes one sentence may be written on several lines in a poem. Point out the different types of punctuation they will encounter as they read the poem. Review the semicolon and that it signals the reader to pause. You may wish to model by reading the first stanza aloud. Invite a volunteer to read the second stanza.

Develop Oral Language

Have students work in pairs to take turns reading every other stanza. Ask them to change stanzas on a second reading.

Writing

Have students choose a constellation, briefly study it, and write an acrostic poem about the constellation. For example, if they chose Orion, have the student write the letters O, R, I, O, N down the left-hand side of a sheet of paper. Tell students that the first line of the poem will begin with O, the second with R, and so on.

Name _____   Date _____

Escape at Bedtime
by Robert Louis Stevenson

The lights from the parlor and kitchen shone out
    Through the blinds and the windows and bars;
And high overhead and all moving about,
    There were thousands of millions of stars.
There never were such thousands of leaves on a tree,
    Nor of people in church or the park,
As the crowds of the stars that looked down upon me,
    And that glittered and winked in the dark.

The Dog, and the Plough, and the Hunter, and all,
    And the star of the sailor, and Mars,
These shone in the sky, and the pail by the wall
    Would be half full of water and stars.
They saw me at last, and they chased me with cries,
    And they soon had me packed into bed;
But the glory kept shining and bright in my eyes,
    And the stars going round in my head.

Name _____ Date _____

Escape at Bedtime: Assessment

🖋 **Think about the poem. Then answer the questions. Fill in the circle next to the correct answer.**

1. What "glittered and winked in the dark"?
   Ⓐ the water in the pail
   Ⓑ the lights from the parlor
   Ⓒ the poet's eyes
   Ⓓ the stars in the sky

2. Before the poet went to bed, he was
   Ⓐ looking at constellations.
   Ⓑ running away from home.
   Ⓒ spying on his family.
   Ⓓ walking to church.

3. A word that means the same as "glory" in this poem would be
   Ⓐ excitement.
   Ⓑ splendor.
   Ⓒ stars.
   Ⓓ memory.

4. Another good title for this poem might be
   Ⓐ "Parlor Lights."
   Ⓑ "Afraid of the Dark."
   Ⓒ "Stars upon Stars."
   Ⓓ "Sleepless."

5. Where is the poet in the beginning of the poem?
   Ⓐ in his room
   Ⓑ in the parlor
   Ⓒ outside
   Ⓓ at the park

6. The poet must be
   Ⓐ a young child.
   Ⓑ an astronomer.
   Ⓒ an old man.
   Ⓓ an infant.

7. The poet wrote, "They saw me at last, and they chased me with cries, / And they soon had me packed into bed." Explain what he was trying to tell the reader.

_____

_____

_____

_____

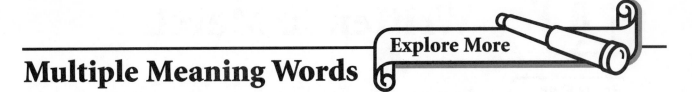

Multiple Meaning Words

Explore More

Some words have more than one meaning. You can use clues in the sentence to tell which meaning the word has.

Example: produce
Meaning A: fresh fruit and vegetables. We bought **produce** at the market.
Meaning B: to bring forth. We watched the magician **produce** a rabbit out of thin air!

Write the letter of the correct meaning next to each sentence.

stars
Meaning A: points of light in the night sky
Meaning B: outstanding or famous performers

_____ 1. The stars were photographed as they walked down the red carpet.

_____ 2. The night sky was full of stars that glittered and winked.

glory
Meaning A: great honor or praise
Meaning B: great beauty or splendor

_____ 3. The glory of the beautiful night sky would stay in my mind forever.

_____ 4. The crowd of villagers gave glory to the king for being such a great leader.

packed
Meaning A: to have placed one's belongings in boxes for storage
Meaning B: to send off quickly

_____ 5. The parents packed the two children off to bed without any warning.

_____ 6. He packed all of his winter clothing and put it away for another year.

Written in March

Vocabulary

twitter–chirp
doth–does
defeated–lost a battle
retreated–gone back
anon–again
prevailing–most common
fountain–a natural spring of water

Research Base

"Students who are immersed in the vibrant sounds of poetry will write better poetry themselves; what's more, they are more likely to develop a lifetime appreciation for poetry." *(Guiding Readers and Writers: Grades 3–6, p. 419)*

Summary

The poet wrote this poem while he was resting on the bridge at a place called Brother's Water in 1802. He describes the scene he observed.

Read the Poem

Introduce the Poem
Invite students to tell about a scene they recall. Tell students that they are going to read a poem about a scene the poet observed.

Introduce the Vocabulary
Write several sets of vocabulary words on index cards. Pass them out so that each student has a word. Write each word on the board and say the word. Give the definition. Ask students holding that card to form a group. After all words have been discussed, ask each group to write a sentence using the word.

After Reading

Questions
1. What does the poet mean when he says, "The green field sleeps in the sun"? (*He means that the sun is shining down on the field that is lying flat as if in sleep.*)
2. What different types of water does the poet name? (*stream, lake, snow, fountains, rain*)
3. What is the overall mood of the poem? (*happy and joyous*)

Fluency
Have students work with a partner to practice reading the poem fluently. Once they feel comfortable reading the poem, have students tape-record themselves reading the poem.

Develop Oral Language
Invite partners to read the poem, alternating lines.

Writing

Review the characteristics of a simile with students. Have students write five sentences that contain similes.

Read the Poem

Written in March
by William Wordsworth

The cock is crowing,
The stream is flowing,
The small birds twitter,
The lake doth glitter,
The green field sleeps in the sun;
The oldest and youngest
Are at work with the strongest;
The cattle are grazing,
Their heads never raising;
There are forty feeding like one!
Like an army defeated
The snow hath retreated,
And now doth fare ill
On the top of the bare hill;
The plowboy is whooping—anon—anon:
There's joy in the mountains;
There's life in the fountains;
Small clouds are sailing,
Blue sky prevailing;
The rain is over and gone!

Name _____   Date _____

Written in March: Assessment

🖋 **Think about the poem. Then answer the questions. Fill in the circle next to the correct answer.**

1. What does the poet say is on the top of the hill?
   - Ⓐ cattle
   - Ⓑ snow
   - Ⓒ birds
   - Ⓓ clouds

2. What did the poet hear before he heard small birds twittering?
   - Ⓐ a cow
   - Ⓑ an army
   - Ⓒ a plowboy
   - Ⓓ a rooster

3. "Prevailing" most likely means
   - Ⓐ flowing into.
   - Ⓑ sleeping beside.
   - Ⓒ rising up.
   - Ⓓ taking over.

4. The main idea of this poem is that
   - Ⓐ when the rain is over in March, everything is better.
   - Ⓑ nothing is as important as work.
   - Ⓒ cattle are too busy eating to look around.
   - Ⓓ March is the best time to write.

5. The season of this poem is
   - Ⓐ winter.
   - Ⓑ spring.
   - Ⓒ summer.
   - Ⓓ fall.

6. It seems that the poet
   - Ⓐ is always in a good mood.
   - Ⓑ owns a lot of land.
   - Ⓒ is a keen observer of his surroundings.
   - Ⓓ plows fields all day long.

7. What does the poet mean when he says that the snow "doth fare ill/On the top of the bare hill"?

_____

_____

_____

Antonyms

Antonyms are words with opposite meanings.
Examples: loss—gain   open—close

Match the words in the box with their antonyms listed below.
Write the words on the line.

| oldest never defeated retreated bare joy small prevailing |

_____ **1.** advanced

_____ **2.** always

_____ **3.** covered

_____ **4.** large

_____ **5.** losing

_____ **6.** sadness

_____ **7.** victorious

_____ **8.** youngest

Choose four pairs of antonyms from above and write a sentence using each pair.

_____

_____

_____

_____

A Happy Man

Poetry Skill: Rhyming Words

Standard
Identify rhyme in poetry

Explore Rhyming Words
The poet used couplets to develop a very predictable rhyme pattern. Remind students that a couplet is two lines of poetry that work together. Most couplets have a rhyme scheme of "aa." Explain that in each stanza of this poem the first two lines, or couplet, have the rhyming "a" pattern, and the second two lines have a "b" pattern. Have students use their copy of the poem to mark the rhyme pattern of each stanza.

Vocabulary

graven–carved or engraved
mournful–feeling or expressing sadness
pity–having feelings of sympathy or sorrow for other people
region–a specific area or space
sorrow–mental suffering of pain caused by injury or loss

Summary

A dead man tells of how happy his life was while he was alive.

Read the Poem

Introduce the Poem

Discuss the meaning of the word *content*. Have students think of things that make them feel happy or content. Point out that the poet wrote the poem to express a certain mood (state of emotion). The poem is about a man who has died. He is telling a stranger about the people and events from his life. Challenge students to identify his mood throughout the poem.

Introduce the Vocabulary

Write the vocabulary words on the board. Discuss the definition of each word.

After Reading

Questions

1. How did the man describe his relationship with his children and his wife? (*He felt they were kind. He was close to them.*)
2. What did the man do while he was alive that he was "happy" about? (*watched his sons marry, rocked his grandsons*)
3. What mood or feeling is the poet describing in this poem? (*Answers may vary. Possible response: a mood of happiness and contentmen*t)

Fluency

Direct the students to look at the last stanza. There is an em dash at the end of the second line. Explain that an em dash signals a change in thought. It is commonly used where a period is too strong and a comma is too weak. Model how to read the last stanza for the students. Then invite partners to practice reading the last stanza of the poem.

Develop Oral Language

Invite students to work as partners. One student reads the lines that have the "a" rhyming pattern, and the partner reads the lines with the "b" rhyming pattern. Then have partners switch lines.

Writing

Have the students think of a mood that they would like to describe in a poem. It may be any feeling from pride or joy to sorrow or anger. Have them write a poem with an "aabb" rhyme pattern about this mood. Encourage them to use describing words and events to help tell about the mood. Ask volunteers to read their poems to the class and have the other students guess the mood of each poem.

A Happy Man
by Edwin Arlington Robinson

When these graven lines you see,
Traveler, do not pity me;
Though I be among the dead,
Let no mournful word be said.

Children that I leave behind,
And their children, all were kind;
Near to them and to my wife,
I was happy all my life.

My three sons I married right,
And their sons I rocked at night;
Death nor sorrow ever brought
Cause for one unhappy thought.

Now, and with no need of tears,
Here they leave me, full of years,—
Leave me to my quiet rest
In the region of the blest.

Name _____   Date _____

A Happy Man: Assessment

Think about the poem. Then answer the questions. Fill in the circle next to the correct answer.

1. The man in the poem was
   Ⓐ a traveler before he died.
   Ⓑ old when he died.
   Ⓒ married three times.
   Ⓓ young when he died.

2. After the man raised his three sons,
   Ⓐ he was married.
   Ⓑ he had the joy of holding his grandsons.
   Ⓒ he and his wife had more children.
   Ⓓ he was tired of children.

3. "Mournful" means
   Ⓐ in the morning.
   Ⓑ full of hate.
   Ⓒ old and tired.
   Ⓓ full of sorrow.

4. This poem mostly describes
   Ⓐ a cemetery.
   Ⓑ regrets.
   Ⓒ a happy life.
   Ⓓ a traveler.

5. The poet is "speaking" to
   Ⓐ his children.
   Ⓑ his grandchildren.
   Ⓒ his wife.
   Ⓓ someone passing by.

6. When the man was living, he was most likely
   Ⓐ full of despair.
   Ⓑ very contented.
   Ⓒ a lonely person.
   Ⓓ difficult to be with.

7. Why does the man say that his family has "no need of tears"?

_____

_____

_____

_____

Dictionary Skills

Explore More

A dictionary tells how to say a word and what it means.

Look at the pronunciation key. Circle the word that matches the pronunciation. Then write a sentence for each word that you circled.

a	add	i	it	o͝o	took	oi	oil
ā	ace	ī	ice	o͞o	pool	ou	pout
â	care	o	odd	u	up	ng	ring
ä	palm	ō	open	û	burn	th	thin
e	end	ô	order	yo͞o	fuse	th	this
ē	equal					zh	vision

ə = { a in *above*   e in *sicken*   i in *possible*
      o in *melon*   u in *circus* }

1. (pit´ē)   party   pity   pretty

_____

2. (rē´jən)   reaching   reason   region

_____

3. (grā´vən)   grave   graven   gravy

_____

4. (sôr´ō)   sorrow   sorry   sore

_____

5. (môrn´fəl)   mindful   misrule   mournful

_____

6. (ə mung´)   amend   among   amongst

_____

7. (deth)   deaf   death   dead

_____

8. (trav´əl ər)   travel   travels   traveler

_____

Three Thoughts of My Heart

Poetry Skill: Personification

Standard
Identify the use of figurative language (personification)

Explore Personification
Explain to students that some poets use personification in order to give human qualities to an animal or an object. For example, in this poem the poet has given her heart the thoughts and words of a person. Practice using personification with students by writing the names of everyday objects and animals on pieces of paper. Put them in a container and have volunteers draw a name. Challenge the class to work together to personify the name drawn. Example: the moon—the moon stared down at me

Vocabulary

brook–a small natural stream of fresh water
content–satisfied with what one has; not wanting more or anything else
cushion–a soft pillow or pad
moss–tiny, soft plants that usually grow in patches on moist ground
straying–wandering or roaming

Summary

The poet gives her heart the ability to "speak" and "think" in this free verse poem.

Read the Poem

Introduce the Poem
Ask students if they have ever had to make a difficult decision. Invite volunteers to share how they usually make difficult decisions. Explain that sometimes people will tell you "to simply listen to your heart" when you are making a decision. Ask students if they believe our heart really talks to us. Explain that in the poem we are reading the poet believes it does. She has given her heart the ability to think and speak in this poem.

Introduce the Vocabulary
Write the vocabulary words and the definitions on the board. Have students give examples of sentences using the new words.

After Reading

Questions
1. What three thoughts does the poet's heart have for her? (*a thought of clouds, a thought of birds, a thought of flowers*)
2. What does the poet ask her heart? (*"What would you do . . . If you were a floating ship of the sky . . . If you were a peering bird . . . If you were a wild geranium?"*)
3. What do the thoughts that the poet's heart has and the questions that the poet asks her heart have to do with one another? (*Answers will vary. Possible response: each thought creates a question*)

Fluency
Discuss with students the use of ellipsis points in each stanza of this poem. Explain that ellipsis points are three dots used to show the omission of a word or words. They signal the reader to pause. Model how to read the poem. Then ask partners to practice reading it.

Develop Oral Language
Have students alternate reading the stanzas.

Writing

Have students think about cartoon animals that they watch on television. Explain that these animals are good examples of personification because they have been given human traits and emotions. Challenge students to draw their own cartoon animals and write sentences that personify their animal.

Name _____   Date _____

Three Thoughts of My Heart
by Hilda Conkling

As I was straying by the forest brook
I heard my heart speak to me:
Listen, said my heart,
I have three thoughts for you . . .
A thought of clouds,
A thought of birds,
A thought of flowers.

I sat upon a cushion of moss,
Listening,
Where the light played, and the green shadows:
What would you do . . . I asked my heart . . .
If you were a floating ship of the sky . . .
If you were a peering bird . . .
If you were a wild geranium?

And my heart made answer:
That is what I wonder and wonder!
After all it is life I love,
After all I am a living thing,
After all I am the heart of you . . .
I am content!

Understand the Poem

Three Thoughts of My Heart: Assessment

Think about the poem. Then answer the questions. Fill in the circle next to the correct answer.

1. What speaks to the poet?
   - Ⓐ her friend
   - Ⓑ a bird
   - Ⓒ a flower
   - Ⓓ her heart

2. The poet is spoken to
   - Ⓐ as she walks by a brook.
   - Ⓑ after she leaves the brook.
   - Ⓒ when she sits on the moss.
   - Ⓓ before she sees the brook.

3. The poet's heart is content. "Content" means
   - Ⓐ inside.
   - Ⓑ yearning.
   - Ⓒ satisfied.
   - Ⓓ beating.

4. This poem is mostly about
   - Ⓐ a girl's feelings about nature.
   - Ⓑ a girl's thoughts to herself.
   - Ⓒ a girl running away from home.
   - Ⓓ a girl who is looking for change.

5. You can conclude that
   - Ⓐ it is a quiet, sunny day.
   - Ⓑ the girl can see the ocean.
   - Ⓒ it is a cloudy day.
   - Ⓓ there are many birds by the brook.

6. Which of these is most likely true?
   - Ⓐ The girl is lost.
   - Ⓑ The girl thinks she hears someone talking.
   - Ⓒ The girl is happy with herself.
   - Ⓓ The girl should not be alone.

7. What does the poet mean when she says, "I heard my heart speak to me"?

_____

_____

_____

_____

 52

Synonyms

A **synonym** is a word that has the same, or almost the same, meaning as another word.

Examples: small—little   happy—glad

✎ **Write the letter of the synonym beside each word.**

_____ **1.** content   **A.** darkness

_____ **2.** answer   **B.** idea

_____ **3.** shadow   **C.** wandering

_____ **4.** thought   **D.** staring

_____ **5.** brook   **E.** stream

_____ **6.** straying   **F.** satisfied

_____ **7.** peering   **G.** reply

_____ **8.** floating   **H.** sailing

✎ **Use each vocabulary word in the box to write a sentence of your own.**

content	straying	peering	shadows

9. _____

_____

_____

_____

The Castle-Builder

Summary

This is a poem written from a father to his son. The father describes the young boy and hopes he will not be changed by getting older. He wants the son to continue dreaming and reaching for those dreams.

Poetry Skill: Rhyming Words

Standard
Identify rhyme in poetry

Explore Rhyming Words
Tell students that this poem has a rhyme pattern of "abab." Have students use markers or highlighters to circle the rhyming word pairs. Have them use one color for lines that end in "a" and another color for lines that end in "b." Have students choose several rhyming word pairs and brainstorm other words that rhyme with each pair.

Vocabulary

dreamy–given to daydreaming
eager–anxious to do or get something
fair–pleasing or delightful to look at
glorified–honored
legends–any stories coming down from the past
manifold–of many kinds; numerous and varied
marvels–things that bring about wonder, admiration, or astonishment
nursery–a room for infants or young children
silken–resembling silk, as in softness
steeds–horses
tender–warm and gentle

Read the Poem

Introduce the Poem

Have the class work in small groups. Give each group a container of building blocks. Set a timer and let students work cooperatively to build a castle. Display the completed castles. Now that they are all "castle-builders," have them listen to the way the poet describes the "castle-builder" in his poem.

Introduce the Vocabulary

Have students work in small groups. Assign each group a vocabulary word to research. Duplicate and distribute the word card from page 11 and dictionaries. Have each group complete a word card and share it with the class. Use students' completed word cards to create a Word Wall.

After Reading

Questions

1. Does the poet paint a picture of the boy for the reader? Give examples of how he describes the boy. (*Yes. Examples will vary. Possible responses: "a gentle boy with soft and silken locks"; "a dreamy boy, with brown and tender eyes"; "a fearless rider on his father's knee"; "an eager listener unto stories told"*)
2. Does the poet feel that the castles that the boy builds with his blocks will be the only ones he builds? (*No, he says he will build other towers when he gets older.*)
3. How does the poet feel about the boy? (*He loves him.*)

Fluency

Explain that many poems have a rhythm, or beat. Model how to read the poem rhythmically. Then invite partners to practice reading the poem with the same rhythm and speed.

Develop Oral Language

Invite students to read the poem chorally.

Writing

Have students think back to when they were in kindergarten. Then have them think of how it is to be in fifth grade. Have students use the Venn diagram on page 12 to compare and contrast kindergarten and fifth grade. Then, have students use the diagram to write a paragraph.

Name _____   Date _____

The Castle-Builder
by Henry Wadsworth Longfellow

A gentle boy, with soft and silken locks,
　　A dreamy boy, with brown and tender eyes,
A castle-builder, with his wooden blocks,
　　And towers that touch imaginary skies.

A fearless rider on his father's knee,
　　An eager listener unto stories told
At the Round Table of the nursery,
　　Of heroes and adventures manifold.

There will be other towers for thee to build;
　　There will be other steeds for thee to ride;
There will be other legends, and all filled
　　With greater marvels and more glorified.

Build on, and make thy castles high and fair,
　　Rising and reaching upward to the skies;
Listen to voices in the upper air,
　　Nor lose thy simple faith in mysteries.

Lesson 11 • The Castle-Builder: Poem
Poetry: Grade 5, SV 9895-7

Name _____   Date _____

The Castle-Builder: Assessment

🪶— **Think about the poem. Then answer the questions. Fill in the circle next to the correct answer.**

1. What does the boy in the poem ride?
   Ⓐ his father's knee
   Ⓑ a horse
   Ⓒ a train
   Ⓓ a toy

2. When will the boy build "other towers" and ride "other steeds"?
   Ⓐ the next day
   Ⓑ after dinner
   Ⓒ when he is older
   Ⓓ before he hears a story

3. "Manifold" probably means
   Ⓐ frightening.
   Ⓑ unbelievable.
   Ⓒ without end.
   Ⓓ of many kinds.

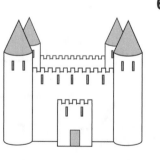

4. The main idea of this poem is that
   Ⓐ the boy needs practice building stronger towers.
   Ⓑ boys should spend time with their fathers.
   Ⓒ a boy's work is never done.
   Ⓓ the father hopes his boy will not change as he grows older.

5. Most likely, this is a poem
   Ⓐ from a mother to her son.
   Ⓑ from a father to his daughter.
   Ⓒ from a father to his son.
   Ⓓ from a grandfather to his grandson.

6. Which of these is probably true?
   Ⓐ The poet is very fond of the boy.
   Ⓑ The poet feels that children waste a lot of time.
   Ⓒ The poet wants the boy to grow up quickly.
   Ⓓ The poet likes to build block castles, too.

7. Why do you think the father hopes his boy will not change as he grows older?

_____

_____

_____

_____

Multiple Meaning Words

Some words have more than one meaning. You can use clues in the sentence to tell which meaning the word has.

Example: ship
Meaning A: a large boat. A **ship** sails across the ocean.
Meaning B: to send or mail large things. The store will **ship** the large box.

Write the letter of the correct meaning next to each sentence.

nursery
Meaning A: a room or area in a household set apart for the use and care of babies
Meaning B: a place where plants are grown under controlled conditions

_____ 1. The nursery was painted a pale shade of blue in preparation for the arrival of the new baby.

_____ 2. Our nursery grows and sells plants that are native to our area.

fair
Meaning A: observing the rules
Meaning B: pleasing to the eye or beautiful
Meaning C: free of clouds or storms

_____ 3. The weather report called for sunny and fair skies.

_____ 4. The coach asked the players to keep the football game friendly and fair.

_____ 5. The fair maiden was considered to be one of the most attractive women in the kingdom.

LESSON 12

Johnson's Boy

Summary

This poem is about a young boy who is always blamed for mischief. He believes that people blame him just because of his father.

Read the Poem

Introduce the Poem

Ask students to think of a time when they felt that they were being treated unfairly or saw someone else being treated unfairly. Ask volunteers to discuss how they felt. Tell students they are going to read a poem about a boy who feels he is treated unfairly by others.

Introduce the Vocabulary

Write the vocabulary words on the board. Have students use the copy of the poem that they used to highlight examples of dialect in the Poetry Skill section. Ask students to circle vocabulary words that they highlighted on their paper. Write the definitions of the vocabulary words on the board and discuss them with students.

After Reading

Questions

1. Who does the boy believe is "turned ag'in' " him? (*the world, all the people around him*)
2. Who follows the boy every day? (*the farmers*)
3. Why do the "hounds" play him "double"? (*They like to get him into trouble.*)
4. What do you think the poet wants us to feel for the boy? (*He wants us to feel sorry for him.*)

Fluency

Reading this selection might be difficult because of the poet's use of dialect. Help students understand that some of the words are actually contractions; these words use apostrophes to signal that there is a letter or letters missing in the word. Model how to read the first stanza for the students. Then invite volunteers to practice reading the second stanza.

Develop Oral Language

Have partners alternate reading the stanzas of the poem. Challenge them to read the poem the way they think the poet would have the boy read it.

Writing

Have students think of a time when they or someone they know was treated unfairly. Have students write a diary entry about the event. Encourage students to write details about what happened and how they felt.

Lesson 12 • Johnson's Boy: Teacher Information
Poetry: Grade 5, SV 9895-7

Johnson's Boy

by James Whitcomb Riley

The world is turned ag'in' me,
    And people says, "They guess
That nothin' else is in me
    But pure maliciousness!"
I git the blame for doin'
    What other chaps destroy,
And I'm a-goin' to ruin
    Because I'm "Johnson's boy."

THAT ain't my name—I'd ruther
    They'd call me IKE or PAT—
But they've forgot the other—
    And so have I, for that!
I reckon it's as handy,
    When Nibsy breaks his toy,
Or someone steals his candy,
    To say 'twas "JOHNSON'S BOY!"

You can't git any water
    At the pump, and find the spout
So durn chuck-full o' mortar
    That you have to bore it out;
You tackle any scholar
    In Wisdom's wise employ,
And I'll bet you half a dollar
    He'll say it's "Johnson's boy!"

Folks don't know how I suffer
    In my uncomplainin' way—
They think I'm gittin' tougher
    And tougher every day.
Last Sunday night, when Flinder
    Was a-shoutin' out for joy,
And someone shook the winder,
    He prayed for "Johnson's boy."

I'm tired of bein' follered
    By farmers every day,
And then o' bein' collared
    For coaxin' hounds away;
Hounds always plays me double—
    It's a trick they all enjoy—
To git me into trouble,
    Because I'm "Johnson's boy."

But if I git to Heaven,
    I hope the Lord'll see
SOME boy has been perfect,
    And lay it on to me;
I'll swell the song sonorous,
    And clap my wings for joy,
And sail off on the chorus—
    "Hurrah for 'Johnson's boy!'"

Johnson's Boy: Assessment

Understand the Poem

🪶— **Think about the poem. Then answer the questions. Fill in the circle next to the correct answer.**

1. What is the boy's real name in the poem?
   Ⓐ Johnson
   Ⓑ He doesn't remember.
   Ⓒ Nibsy
   Ⓓ Ike

2. What happens right after Nibsy breaks his toy?
   Ⓐ The pump will not pump water.
   Ⓑ "Johnson's Boy" is chased by hounds.
   Ⓒ People blame "Johnson's Boy."
   Ⓓ Nibsy cries.

3. What is "maliciousness"?
   Ⓐ meanness
   Ⓑ rudeness
   Ⓒ distrust
   Ⓓ carelessness

4. This story is mostly about
   Ⓐ a boy who cannot stay out of trouble.
   Ⓑ a group of boys who misbehave.
   Ⓒ a boy who misbehaves and has no friends.
   Ⓓ an innocent boy who is blamed for everything.

5. What might you conclude about the boy's father, "Johnson"?
   Ⓐ He was probably a troublemaker.
   Ⓑ People picked on him unfairly, too.
   Ⓒ He is around to defend his son.
   Ⓓ He was an unlucky man.

6. The people in this poem would probably agree with which saying?
   Ⓐ You can't know a person until you walk a mile in his shoes.
   Ⓑ Don't judge a book by its cover.
   Ⓒ The apple doesn't fall far from the tree.
   Ⓓ Beauty is in the eye of the beholder.

7. Why do you think "Johnson's Boy" always seemed to get into trouble?

_____

_____

_____

Name _____   Date _____

Words Using Apostrophes

Explore More

A contraction is a word made from two smaller words. An apostrophe (') shows that one or more letters are missing in the word.

    Example: you + will = you'll

A writer can also use an apostrophe to show that one or more letters are missing in a word. Poets often do this when writing in dialect.

    Example: goin' = going

Read each sentence. Look at the words in dark print. Write each sentence, rewriting each word in dark print correctly without the apostrophe.

1. It seems that **I'm** always blamed for what others do!

_____

_____

2. There were many people **ag'in'** the children misbehaving in town.

_____

_____

3. When Nibsy broke his toy **'twas** the boy's fault again.

_____

_____

4. **They've** even forgotten the boy's name!

_____

_____

5. The town knows **it's** not fair to blame him for every trick **that's** played.

_____

_____

Lesson 12 • **Johnson's Boy:** Vocabulary Skill
Poetry: Grade 5, SV 9895-7

The Children's Hour

Poetry Skill: Metaphor

Standard
Identify the use of figurative language (metaphor)

Explore Metaphor
Discuss that a metaphor shows comparison without the use of *like* or *as*. In a metaphor, the writer says one thing is another thing. Pass out the poem and lead students in a discussion of Longfellow's use of metaphor. Explain that Longfellow writes about the father's home as if it is a castle. He gives the different areas of the house names that are parts of a castle.

Vocabulary

banditti–bandits
depart–to leave
devour–to eat greedily
entwine–to weave together
fortress–a place built with walls and defenses
lamplight–the light cast by a lamp
occupations–jobs or work

Research Base

"**P**oetry is a microcosm for learning. Through the precise, concise language of poetry, students learn a lot about reading and writing." (*Guiding Readers and Writers: Grades 3–6, p. 421*)

Summary

This poem is about a special time of the day for a father and his children. During "The Children's Hour," the poet's three girls "attack" their father with love and laughter. The poet paints a picture of a daily occurrence that he enjoys with his children and will remember forever.

Read the Poem

Introduce the Poem
Display a book that has pictures of castles. Ask students to share information that they know about castles. Remind students that although castles were built as defenses against attack, they were also places where people lived. Read the poem aloud and ask students to listen for ways that the poet compares his home to a castle.

Introduce the Vocabulary
Write the vocabulary words and the definitions on the board. Lead students in a brief discussion of the words. Then have students create a crossword puzzle with the words using graph paper. Challenge students to write sentences as clues to complete the puzzle.

After Reading

Questions
1. What do the girls do before they run in and "attack" their father? (*Possible responses: They whisper in the hall. They plot and plan together.*)
2. Who are the "blue-eyed banditti"? (*the poet's children*)
3. Who is the "old mustache"? (*the poet or the children's father*)
4. Do you think the children do this kind of thing often? (*yes*)

Fluency
Tell students that one sentence may be written on several lines in a poem. Point out that the punctuation helps the reader decide how to read each sentence. Point out the exclamation marks that are in the poem. Explain that exclamation points tell the reader to show excitement or expression when reading those lines. Have students practice reading the poem fluently.

Develop Oral Language
Have students work in small groups to take turns reading the stanzas of the poem. Challenge groups to perform the poem.

Writing

Have students write a paragraph describing a special time of the day or daily event that takes place at their home. Challenge students to use words that also compare their home to a castle as the poem does.

The Children's Hour
by Henry Wadsworth Longfellow

Between the dark and the daylight,
   When the night is beginning to lower,
Comes a pause in the day's occupations,
   That is known as the Children's Hour.

I hear in the chamber above me
   The patter of little feet,
The sound of a door that is opened,
   And voices soft and sweet.

From my study I see in the lamplight,
   Descending the broad hall stair,
Grave Alice, and laughing Allegra,
   And Edith with golden hair.

A whisper, and then a silence:
   Yet I know by their merry eyes
They are plotting and planning together
   To take me by surprise.

A sudden rush from the stairway,
   A sudden raid from the hall!
By three doors left unguarded
   They enter my castle wall!

They climb up into my turret
   Over the arms and back of my chair;
If I try to escape, they surround me;
   They seem to be everywhere.

They almost devour me with kisses,
   Their arms about me entwine,
Till I think of the Bishop of Bingen
   In his Mouse-Tower on the Rhine!

Do you think, O blue-eyed banditti,
   Because you have scaled the wall,
Such an old mustache as I am
   Is not a match for you all!

I have you fast in my fortress,
   And will not let you depart,
But put you down into the dungeon
   In the round-tower of my heart.

And there will I keep you forever,
   Yes, forever and a day,
Till the walls shall crumble to ruin,
   And molder in dust away!

Understand the Poem

The Children's Hour: Assessment

Think about the poem. Then answer the questions. Fill in the circle next to the correct answer.

1. When does this poem take place?
ⓐ in the morning
ⓑ in the evening
ⓒ in the middle of the day
ⓓ late at night

2. What happens first?
ⓐ There is a sudden rush from the hallway.
ⓑ There is whispering in the hall.
ⓒ The poet "captures" the children.
ⓓ The poet hears footsteps above.

3. Which of these has the same meaning as "devour"?
ⓐ cover
ⓑ contain
ⓒ consume
ⓓ create

4. Another good name for this poem might be
ⓐ "In the Ruins."
ⓑ "Golden-Haired Edith."
ⓒ "Disturbing Father."
ⓓ "A Father's Fortress."

5. The children have probably
ⓐ never done this type of thing.
ⓑ been afraid to bother their father.
ⓒ tried to surprise their father this way at other times.
ⓓ been punished for interrupting their father in his study.

6. Which of these seems true of the father?
ⓐ He enjoys the company of his daughters.
ⓑ He is annoyed by the noises children make.
ⓒ He does not have time for foolishness.
ⓓ He wishes he could lock his children away.

7. Why do you think the poet chose "The Children's Hour" as the title for this poem?

_____

_____

_____

Name _____   Date _____

Compound Words

A **compound word** is a word made by putting two or more words together.
   Examples: sunrise, moonlit

Join one word from Column A with one word from Column B to make a compound word. Write the new words.

Column A

stair

lamp

day

for

every

over

Column B

light

ever

way

joyed

light

where

1. _____

2. _____

3. _____

4. _____

5. _____

6. _____

Dictionary Skills

The words in a dictionary are listed in **alphabetical order.**
   Example: read, school, spelling, success

Write the compound words from above in alphabetical order.

7. _____

8. _____

9. _____

10. _____

11. _____

12. _____

Mother to Son

Poetry Skill: Metaphor

Standard
Identify the use of figurative language (metaphor)

Explore Metaphor
Tell students that a metaphor makes a comparison without the use of *like* or *as*. In a metaphor, the writer says one thing *is* another thing. Pass out the poem. Read the poem aloud and help students understand that Langston Hughes compares the "ups and downs" of the mother's life to a damaged staircase. Use the Venn diagram from page 12 to compare the characteristics of life and a staircase. Explain to students that the poet used this strong metaphor in order to create a mental image for the reader.

Vocabulary

ain't–has not
bare–without covering
goin'–going
kinder–kind of

Research Base

"**Poetry** is an essential, integral part of the language/literacy curriculum . . . ." (*Guiding Readers and Writers: Grades 3–6, p. 414*)

Summary

The poem tells of a mother telling her son about her life. She tells him that life can be difficult at times; however, he must never give up no matter how hard things get.

Read the Poem

Introduce the Poem
Introduce the word *goal*. Discuss what this word means. Ask students for examples of goals that they might have. Lead students in a discussion about times in their life when they have had difficulty reaching a goal. Tell them that this poem is about a mother who wants her son to understand that life can be difficult sometimes; however, she also tells him that he should never give up trying to reach his goals.

Introduce the Vocabulary
Write the vocabulary words on the board. Tell students that some of the vocabulary words are examples of words written in dialect. Discuss all the words with the students. Write the definitions on the board.

After Reading

Questions
1. What does the mother mean when she warns the boy about the stair having "tacks in it, and splinters, and boards torn up"? (*She means that life has things that can be dangerous in it. You have to watch out for these things.*)
2. The mother says, "I'se been a-climbin' on." What does she mean? (*She has continued to reach for her goals.*)

Fluency
Discuss the use of apostrophes to replace missing letters in words. Tell students that this is a common practice when using dialect in writing. Model reading the poem to the students. Then have partners rehearse the poem several times.

Develop Oral Language
Explain that dialect can make it difficult to read poetry aloud. Challenge volunteers to perform a "retelling" of the poem, replacing dialect with standard English. Have partners alternate reading the stanzas.

Writing

Have students write a paragraph about a time in their lives when they didn't "set down on the steps" (didn't give up no matter how hard it got). Ask volunteers to share their experiences.

Mother to Son
by Langston Hughes

Well, son, I'll tell you,
Life for me ain't been no crystal stair.
It's had tacks in it,
And splinters,
And boards torn up,
And places with no carpet on the floor—
Bare.

But all the time
I'se been a-climbin' on,
And reachin' landin's,
And turnin' corners,
And sometimes goin' in the dark
Where there ain't been no light.

So, boy, don't you turn back.
Don't you set down on the steps
'Cause you find it kinder hard.
Don't you fall now—
For I'se still goin', honey,
I'se still climbin',
And life for me ain't been no
crystal stair.

Understand the Poem

Mother to Son: Assessment

✎ **Think about the poem. Then answer the questions. Fill in the circle next to the correct answer.**

1. The mother says that life for her "ain't been no crystal stair" because life
   - Ⓐ has not been easy.
   - Ⓑ has been too long.
   - Ⓒ has taught her you need a lot of friends.
   - Ⓓ has not been hard.

2. What is the first thing the mother tells her son?
   - Ⓐ Sometimes she has traveled in the dark.
   - Ⓑ Don't give up.
   - Ⓒ Life has sometimes been bare.
   - Ⓓ None of the above

3. Why is the mother afraid that the son might "set down on the steps"?
   - Ⓐ He might be too lazy to go on.
   - Ⓑ He might find life too hard.
   - Ⓒ He might not see where he is going.
   - Ⓓ He might be able to tell the future.

4. What is the main message of this poem?
   - Ⓐ Don't rely on others to help you.
   - Ⓑ The goal is not worth the effort.
   - Ⓒ You can always count on family to help you through difficult times.
   - Ⓓ Don't give up no matter what.

5. What was the author's purpose in writing this poem?
   - Ⓐ to tell the boy's life story
   - Ⓑ to describe a staircase
   - Ⓒ to teach readers a lesson
   - Ⓓ to entertain readers

6. What trait does the mother have that she hopes her son will also develop?
   - Ⓐ loyalty
   - Ⓑ honesty
   - Ⓒ kindness
   - Ⓓ determination

7. The mother says, "Don't you fall now—." What is she really telling her son?

_____

_____

_____

Words Using Apostrophes

A contraction is a word made from two smaller words. An apostrophe (') shows that one or more letters are missing in the word.

Example: you + will = you'll

A writer can also use an apostrophe to show that one or more letters are missing in a word. Poets often do this when writing in dialect.

Example: goin' = going

Read each sentence. Look at the words in dark print. Write each sentence, rewriting each word in dark print correctly without the apostrophe.

1. The mother said, "**I'll** tell you that life can be difficult at times."

   _____

   _____

2. She wanted her son to continue **reachin'** for his dreams.

   _____

   _____

3. **It's** not always easy to reach for your dreams.

   _____

   _____

4. **Don't** let difficult things keep you from working toward a goal.

   _____

   _____

5. Even when things seem impossible, keep **goin'** towards your goal.

   _____

   _____

Portrait by a Neighbour

Summary

The poet describes the odd and entertaining habits of her carefree neighbor.

Poetry Skill: Simile

Standard

Identify the use of figurative language (simile)

Explore Simile

Explain to the students that one of the ways a poet can show comparison is through the use of similes. A simile is a comparison of two things using the words *like* or *as*. Have students highlight the similes in the poem. Discuss the meaning of the comparisons that this poet has made.

Vocabulary

borrowed–got something from another person by agreeing to return it later
meadow–grassland or pasture used for growing hay
portrait–a verbal picture or description

Teacher Tips

Point out the variant spelling of the word *neighbour* with a *u*.

Read the Poem

Introduce the Poem

Introduce the word *portrait* to students. Lead them in a discussion of the word's meaning and how an artist uses paints to create a portrait of someone. Explain to them that the poet has used her words (instead of paints) to "paint" a picture of her carefree neighbor.

Introduce the Vocabulary

Write the vocabulary words on the board. Have students guess what each word means. Write students' guesses on the board. Then, have students look up the words in the dictionary. Write the definition for each word on the board.

After Reading

Questions

1. What does the poet say about the neighbor's lawn? (*She doesn't mow often and when she does, she does not do a very thorough job.*)
2. What do you think the poet is trying to say about her neighbor when she writes, "It's long after midnight/Her key's in the lock"? (*Possible response: The neighbor is forgetful.*)
3. Does the poet enjoy living next to the neighbor? (*Answers will vary.*)

Fluency

Point out to students that this poem has line breaks that do not have end punctuation. Remind them that when there is no end punctuation, they should continue to read the sentence smoothly and fluently. Direct students' attention to the exclamation marks. Explain that these mean that they should read with an excited expression. Have students practice reading the poem fluently.

Develop Oral Language

Assign five students to a group. Have each student in the group choose and read one of the stanzas.

Writing

Have students "paint" a portrait with words of one of their neighbors or someone they see frequently. Have them write a paragraph describing this person's physical appearance and the things they observe the person doing. Challenge students to use similes in their description. Have them draw a portrait to match their description.

Name _____   Date _____

Portrait by a Neighbour
by Edna St. Vincent Millay

Before she has her floor swept
Or her dishes done,
Any day you'll find her
A-sunning in the sun!

It's long after midnight
Her key's in the lock,
And you never see her chimney smoke
Till past ten o'clock!

She digs in her garden
With a shovel and a spoon,
She weeds her lazy lettuce
By the light of the moon.

She walks up the walk
Like a woman in a dream,
She forgets she borrowed butter
And pays you back in cream!

Her lawn looks like a meadow,
And if she mows the place
She leaves the clover standing
And the Queen Anne's lace!

Portrait by a Neighbour: Assessment

Understand the Poem

✎—— **Think about the poem. Then answer the questions. Fill in the circle next to the correct answer.**

1. The poet says that if the neighbor borrows butter she will
   Ⓐ never pay you back.
   Ⓑ forget that you live next door.
   Ⓒ pay you back in cream.
   Ⓓ leave butter on your doorstep.

2. What does the neighbor do before she has swept her floor?
   Ⓐ She does her dishes.
   Ⓑ She suns herself.
   Ⓒ She mows her lawn.
   Ⓓ She weeds her garden.

3. The poem says, "She walks up the walk/Like a woman in a dream." The poet makes this comparison to describe how her neighbor
   Ⓐ sleepwalks during the day.
   Ⓑ always walks slowly.
   Ⓒ has many dreams.
   Ⓓ is often lost in her own thoughts.

4. If this poem needed a new title, which title would be BEST?
   Ⓐ "In the Garden"
   Ⓑ "The Unusual Woman Next Door"
   Ⓒ "A Lawn Like a Meadow"
   Ⓓ "Lazy Days of Summer"

5. What does the first stanza tell you about the poet's neighbor?
   Ⓐ She is a neat person.
   Ⓑ She does her chores right away.
   Ⓒ She is a carefree person.
   Ⓓ She is a restless person.

6. It is clear that the poet wrote this poem
   Ⓐ to entertain readers with the things her neighbor does.
   Ⓑ to instruct readers on how to be a good neighbor.
   Ⓒ to persuade readers to like her neighbor.
   Ⓓ to show how her neighbor does her gardening.

7. The poet writes, "She walks up the walk/Like a woman in a dream." The poet is making a comparison by using a simile. How do you know that this sentence is a simile?

_____

_____

_____

Name _____   Date _____

Word Puzzle

Read each sentence. Choose a word from the box that correctly completes each sentence. Write the word in the puzzle.

| portrait | meadow | sunning | neighbor | borrowed | chimney |

Across

2. You will always find my neighbor _____ outside instead of completing her household chores.

4. If I were to draw a _____ of my neighbor, her face would have a content smile.

5. Smoke never rises from the neighbor's _____ until late at night.

Down

1. Once my neighbor _____ butter and absent-mindedly returned cream to me.

3. By looking at the yard next door, you can tell that my _____ is not a very tidy person.

6. Her yard always looks like a _____ that you might see while taking a nature walk.

Lesson 15 • Portrait by a Neighbour: Vocabulary Skill
Poetry: Grade 5, SV 9895-7

[from] Our Hero

Summary

This is the story of a hero who shows true courage in helping save a ship and its passengers from a fiery end.

Read the Poem

Introduce the Poem

Introduce the word *hero*. Ask students what it means to be a hero. Lead them in a discussion about the qualities it takes to be a hero. Have students listen to the poem for the qualities that a hero might demonstrate.

Introduce the Vocabulary

Write the vocabulary words on the board. Have students work in pairs. Assign each pair of students one of the vocabulary words to research. Ask students to look for the word in the dictionary, write a definition for the word, and use the word in a sentence. Have each pair of students present the information they have collected. Invite students to write their definition on the board as they present their information.

After Reading

Activity

Have students work in pairs to complete the story map on page 13. Use the story maps to discuss the elements of the story being told by the poet.

Fluency

Point out that many poems have a rhythm, or beat. Then model how to read the poem rhythmically. Point out the em dash in the fifth stanza. Tell students that an em dash signals a pause. Have students practice reading the poem to develop fluency.

Develop Oral Language

Have students work in groups to practice reading or acting out this poem.

Writing

Have students work in small groups to write a short play or skit to go with this poem. Ask them to create a list of the actors, the setting, and the props to be used. Challenge them to write the dialogue for each actor and the directions for what the actors should be doing when they are speaking. Have students perform their play or skit for the class.

Vocabulary

anguish–suffering or pain
fated–doomed
grating–harsh in sound
martyr–a person who sacrifices his life
rapture–joy or delight
strains–melodies or tunes
trod–to step or walk
unfaltering–determined
vacant–empty
valiant–courageous

Name _____   Date _____

[from] Our Hero
by Frances E. W. Harper

While the flames were madly roaring,
With a courage grand and high,
Forth he rushed unto our rescue,
Strong to suffer, brave to die.

Helplessly the boat was drifting,
Death was staring in each face,
When he grasped the fallen rudder,
Took the pilot's vacant place.

Could he save us? Would he save us?
All his hope of life give o'er?
Could he hold that fated vessel
'Till she reached the nearer shore?

All our hopes and fears were centered
'Round his strong, unfaltering hand;
If he failed us we must perish,
Perish just in sight of land.

Breathlessly we watched and waited
While the flames were raging fast;
When our anguish changed to rapture—
We were saved, yes, saved at last.

Never strains of sweetest music
Brought to us more welcome sound
Than the grating of that steamer
When her keel had touched the ground.

But our faithful martyr hero
Through a fiery pathway trod,
Till he laid his valiant spirit
On the bosom of his God.

Fame has never crowned a hero
On the crimson fields of strife,
Grander, nobler, than that pilot
Yielding up for us his life.

[from] Our Hero: Assessment

➤ **Think about the poem. Then answer the questions. Fill in the circle next to the correct answer.**

1. Why was the boat in danger?
- Ⓐ There was a storm.
- Ⓑ There were pirates coming.
- Ⓒ The boat was sinking.
- Ⓓ The boat was on fire.

2. What happened before the "hero" took the rudder?
- Ⓐ The pilot had left it.
- Ⓑ The passengers tried to steer the boat.
- Ⓒ The fire destroyed the boat.
- Ⓓ The passengers begged him for help.

3. Another word for "rapture" is
- Ⓐ surprise.
- Ⓑ dread.
- Ⓒ joy.
- Ⓓ anguish.

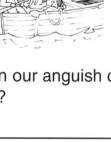

4. This poem is mainly about
- Ⓐ a man who gives his life to save others.
- Ⓑ a ship on fire.
- Ⓒ a steamship.
- Ⓓ the unfortunate pilot.

5. Without the selfless actions of the "hero,"
- Ⓐ someone else would probably have saved the ship.
- Ⓑ the passengers and the boat would have been lost.
- Ⓒ another boat would have come along to save them.
- Ⓓ the ship would probably have run aground eventually.

6. The "hero" could be described as
- Ⓐ brave but foolish.
- Ⓑ strong but unsure.
- Ⓒ courageous and strong.
- Ⓓ rash and careless.

7. The poet writes, "When our anguish changed to rapture—." Why is this line important in the poem?

_____

_____

_____

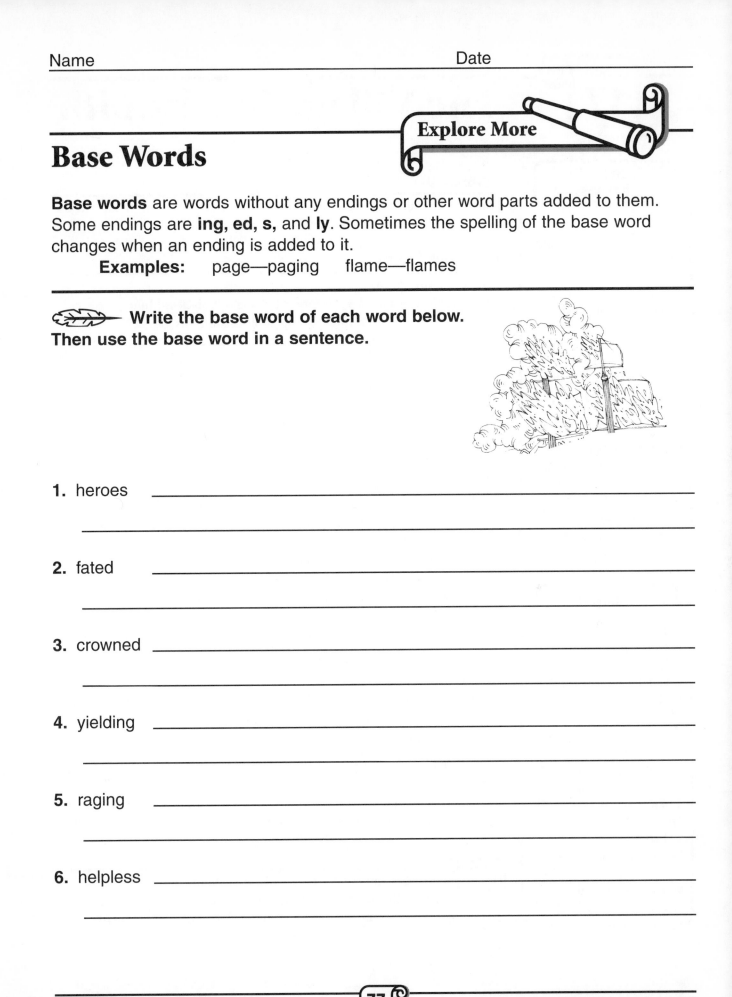

Explore More

Base Words

Base words are words without any endings or other word parts added to them. Some endings are **ing, ed, s,** and **ly**. Sometimes the spelling of the base word changes when an ending is added to it.

   Examples: page—paging flame—flames

✏ **Write the base word of each word below. Then use the base word in a sentence.**

1. heroes _____

_____

2. fated _____

_____

3. crowned _____

_____

4. yielding _____

_____

5. raging _____

_____

6. helpless _____

_____

LESSON 17

The Village Blacksmith

Summary

Longfellow writes this ballad praising a hardworking blacksmith. Longfellow shows how the blacksmith's character has shaped his luck in life.

Poetry Skill: Ballads

Standard
Identify a ballad

Explore Ballads
Tell students that ballads are stories about famous people or events, told in short stanzas. Tell students that writing a ballad is a lot like plotting a story. The stanzas are arranged in chronological order so that the story unfolds in a logical sequence. As the students read the poem, discuss the chronological order. Create a story map on the board to record elements of the story being told in the poem.

Vocabulary

attempted–tried
brawny–strong
forge–a furnace or hearth where metals are heated
hast–have
rejoice–to feel joyful or to be delighted
repose–a rest
sexton–a person who takes care of church property
sinewy–lean and muscular
task–work assigned or done as part of one's duties
toiling–laboring or doing work
wrought–fashioned or shaped

Read the Poem

Introduce the Poem

Introduce the word *blacksmith*. Find a book about blacksmithing to use to discuss the job of a blacksmith and the tools used in this job. Tell students that during the Colonial period blacksmithing was an important job. Explain that the poem is a ballad about a hardworking and honest blacksmith.

Introduce the Vocabulary

Write sentences on the board using each vocabulary word. Challenge students to define each word using context clues.

After Reading

Questions

1. What words does the poet use to describe the blacksmith's physical appearance? (*Possible responses: mighty; large, sinewy hands; brawny arms; hair was crisp, black, and long; tan face; wet, sweaty brow*)
2. What can be heard coming from the blacksmith's shop? (*his bellows and the swinging of the sledge hammer*)
3. What do the children like to do at the blacksmith's shop? (*They love seeing the flaming forge and catching the burning sparks that fly around.*)
4. In the seventh stanza, what does the poet say the blacksmith spends his time doing? (*toiling, rejoicing, sorrowing*)

Fluency

Explain to students that most ballads have a specific rhythm pattern. Model the rhythm of this ballad for students by reading it aloud.

Develop Oral Language

Have students work in small groups to practice reading the ballad aloud. Encourage them to pay attention to the rhythm pattern as they read. Then have students use the tune of a popular song to go with the words of the ballad. Have each group of students perform the ballad for the rest of the class.

Writing

Have students work in pairs to select a historical figure and list some of his or her accomplishments. Next have students arrange the events in chronological order, selecting the most interesting ones. Have student groups use the information gathered to write a ballad.

Name _____   Date _____

The Village Blacksmith
by Henry Wadsworth Longfellow

Under a spreading chestnut-tree
The village smithy stands;
The smith, a mighty man is he,
With large and sinewy hands;
And the muscles of his brawny arms
Are strong as iron bands.

His hair is crisp, and black, and long,
His face is like the tan;
His brow is wet with honest sweat,
He earns whate'er he can,
And looks the whole world in the face,
For he owes not any man.

Week in, week out, from morn till night,
You can hear his bellows blow;
You can hear him swing his heavy sledge,
With measured beat and slow,
Like a sexton ringing the village bell,
When the evening sun is low.

And children coming home from school
Look in at the open door;
They love to see the flaming forge,
And hear the bellows roar,
And catch the burning sparks that fly
Like chaff from a threshing-floor.

He goes on Sunday to the church,
And sits among his boys;
He hears the parson pray and preach,
He hears his daughter's voice,
Singing in the village choir,
And it makes his heart rejoice.

It sounds to him like her mother's voice,
Singing in Paradise!
He needs must think of her once more,
How in the grave she lies;
And with his hard, rough hand he wipes
A tear out of his eyes.

Toiling,–rejoicing,–sorrowing,
Onward through life he goes;
Each morning sees some task begin,
Each evening sees it close;
Something attempted, something done,
Has earned a night's repose.

Thanks, thanks to thee, my worthy friend,
For the lesson thou hast taught!
Thus at the flaming forge of life
Our fortunes must be wrought;
Thus on its sounding anvil shaped
Each burning deed and thought.

The Village Blacksmith: Assessment

Understand the Poem

✎ **Think about the poem. Then answer the questions. Fill in the circle next to the correct answer.**

1. What was the blacksmith's brow wet with?
   Ⓐ honest sweat
   Ⓑ raindrops
   Ⓒ tears
   Ⓓ blood

2. What does the blacksmith think about after hearing his daughter sing?
   Ⓐ He thinks of the work that has to be done.
   Ⓑ He thinks about children coming home from school.
   Ⓒ He thinks of what is for Sunday dinner.
   Ⓓ He thinks about his dead wife.

3. The blacksmith "has earned a night's repose." A "repose" is probably a
   Ⓐ vacation.
   Ⓑ new position.
   Ⓒ rest.
   Ⓓ pay raise.

4. What is the lesson that Longfellow tries to pass on with this ballad?
   Ⓐ Be honest and hardworking during the week.
   Ⓑ Be grateful for everything.
   Ⓒ Our life is shaped by our deeds and thoughts.
   Ⓓ There is a reason for death.

5. What might you conclude about the blacksmith?
   Ⓐ that he doesn't enjoy children
   Ⓑ that he is an honest and hardworking man
   Ⓒ that he takes vacations frequently
   Ⓓ that he sings in the choir

6. Based on Longfellow's description of the blacksmith, which of these adjectives would NOT describe him?
   Ⓐ powerful
   Ⓑ hardworking
   Ⓒ fearful
   Ⓓ responsible

7. Which one of your five senses does Longfellow appeal to in the third stanza of the poem? How do you know which of your senses he is appealing to?

_____

_____

_____

Name _____   Date _____

Synonyms

Explore More

A **synonym** is a word that has the same, or almost the same, meaning as another word.

Examples: small—little   happy—glad

✎ **Write the letter of the synonym beside each word.**

_____ **1.** task

_____ **2.** toil

_____ **3.** brawny

_____ **4.** sinewy

_____ **5.** repose

_____ **6.** rejoice

_____ **7.** wrought

A. rest

B. muscular

C. job

D. celebrate

E. formed

F. strong

G. work

✎ **Use each vocabulary word (1–7) to write a sentence of your own.**

8. _____

9. _____

10. _____

11. _____

12. _____

13. _____

14. _____

Lesson 17 • The Village Blacksmith: Vocabulary Skill
Poetry: Grade 5, SV 9895-7

The Flower

Poetry Skill: Elements of Story Structure

Standard
Identify elements of story structure in fiction and poetry

Explore Elements of Story Structure
Remind students that a poem can tell a story the same way a book can. The poem can describe characters and have a setting, a problem, and events that lead to a solution. Discuss with students that this particular poem is called a fable by the poet. A fable usually ends with a lesson. Many fables are short poems. Ask students to find a lesson in this poem.

Vocabulary

bower–place shaded by trees or shrubs
crown–the top or highest part of something
discontent–uneasiness of mind; dissatisfaction
fro–away; back
muttering–complaining or grumbling
poor–not beautiful
sow'd (sowed)–to have spread or scattered
splendid–magnificent
thro'–contraction for *through*

Summary

This poem is the poet's tale of how he planted a seed. According to the poet, the seed grew into a flower; however, others believed it to be a weed. The seed was stolen and spread about. Then it began to grow all over!

Read the Poem

Introduce the Poem

Show two groups of pictures to students. One group of pictures should contain flowers from a florist and one group should contain pictures of native flowers that most people consider to be weeds. Lead students in a discussion about what makes a flower different from a weed. Ask students which group is more beautiful than the other. Tell students that the poem deals with this very discussion.

Introduce the Vocabulary

Write the vocabulary words and the definitions on the board. Discuss each one with students.

After Reading

Questions

1. What is a fable? (*a short story that is not always true or founded on fact*)
2. Did the poet plant the flowers on purpose? (*yes*)
3. How did the flower begin to grow everywhere? (*The seed was stolen and scattered.*)
4. What does the poet mean when he says the people were "muttering discontent"? (*They were unhappy with the flowers growing everywhere. They made comments complaining about the flowers.*)

Fluency

Model how to read the poem at an appropriate, rhythmic speed. Have pairs of students take turns clapping out the beat as the partner reads.

Develop Oral Language

Have students practice reading the poem to a partner. Then, have them practice retelling the story as if they were talking to a friend. Emphasize that legends and fables usually started out as stories that were simply told. They weren't always written down.

Writing

Share several examples of fables with your students. Have them write their own fable about a lesson they think is important to pass on to others.

The Flower

by Alfred, Lord Tennyson

Once in a golden hour
I cast to earth a seed.
Up there came a flower,
The people said, a weed.

To and fro they went
Thro' my garden bower,
And muttering discontent
Cursed me and my flower.

Then it grew so tall
It wore a crown of light,
But thieves from o'er the wall
Stole the seed by night.

Sow'd it far and wide
By every town and tower,
Till all the people cried,
"Splendid is the flower!"

Read my little fable:
He that runs may read.
Most can raise the flowers now,
For all have got the seed.

And some are pretty enough,
And some are poor indeed;
And now again the people
Call it but a weed.

Understand the Poem

The Flower: Assessment

✏️ **Think about the poem. Then answer the questions. Fill in the circle next to the correct answer.**

1. What was stolen?
   - Ⓐ the flower
   - Ⓑ the seed of the flower
   - Ⓒ the poet's garden
   - Ⓓ some money

2. When did the people praise the flower?
   - Ⓐ before the thieves came over the wall
   - Ⓑ after the thieves came over the wall
   - Ⓒ before the seed was spread far and wide
   - Ⓓ after all the people got the seed

3. The meaning of "poor" at the end of this poem is
   - Ⓐ without money.
   - Ⓑ unhappy.
   - Ⓒ broken.
   - Ⓓ not beautiful.

4. The main idea of this poem is
   - Ⓐ people agree on what is beautiful and what is not.
   - Ⓑ it shouldn't matter what others call a thing if it is beautiful to you.
   - Ⓒ it is easier to grow a weed than it is to grow a flower.
   - Ⓓ having a seed does not mean that you can grow it.

5. The poet probably
   - Ⓐ thought that his flower was beautiful.
   - Ⓑ cared what the people thought of his flower.
   - Ⓒ was ashamed of his flower.
   - Ⓓ grew many weeds in his garden.

6. The flower in this poem could represent
   - Ⓐ children.
   - Ⓑ weather.
   - Ⓒ an idea or belief.
   - Ⓓ other plants.

7. At the beginning of the poem, why do you think the people in the poem didn't agree with the idea that the flower was beautiful?

   _____

   _____

   _____

Words in Context

Use other words in sentences to help you find the missing word.

Read each sentence. Find a word from the box to complete it. Then write the word on the line.

muttered	discontent	crown	cast	poor	splendid

1. She drew her arm back and _____ the seed across the yard in hopes that flowers would grow.

2. When the weeds grew instead of flowers, her neighbors became

   _____ and glared angrily as they passed her yard.

3. She could hear the negative comments that they _____ outside as they passed.

4. Before long, the weeds bloomed a yellow _____ at the top of the stems.

5. The neighbors admired the _____ change that had taken place.

6. The _____ plants with their faded blooms were overshadowed by the beauty of those just starting to bloom.

[from] Paul Revere's Ride

Poetry Skill: Elements of Story Structure

Standard
Identify elements of story structure in fiction and in poetry

Explore Elements of Story Structure
Remind students that a poem can tell a story the same way a book can. The poem can describe characters and have a setting, a problem, and events that lead to a solution. Complete the story map from page 13 as students read this poem.

Vocabulary

aloft–in the air; high above the ground
arm–to equip with weapons to fight
bleating–crying of sheep
borne–carried along
defiance–a challenge to fight
emerge–to rise or come forth
impetuous–sudden or impulsive action
lingers–puts off leaving
peril–exposure to the risk of being injured or destroyed
pierced–made a hole in
sombre–dark and gloomy
spectral–ghostly
steed–a horse
stride–a long step
twitter–light chirping of birds

Summary

This narrative verse is an account of the famous midnight ride of a night watchman named Paul Revere at the beginning of the American Revolution on April 18, 1775.

Read the Poem

Introduce the Poem
Create a transparency from the KWHL chart on page 9. Have students discuss what they already know about Paul Revere and the American Revolution. Tell them the poem is a historical narrative verse based on the famous midnight ride of Paul Revere. Explain that historical narrative verse is based on an historical event; however, the truth sometimes is exaggerated.

Introduce the Vocabulary
Have students work in small groups. Assign each group one vocabulary word. First, ask the groups to guess what the word means. Then, have students use a dictionary to find the definition of the word. Have each group write a sentence using the word. Finally, have each group present its research results.

After Reading

Activity
Use the story map on page 13 to list the elements of this narrative verse. This is a lengthy poem and will need to be read stanza by stanza in order to work through the story map.

Fluency
Point out that in the second stanza there are quotation marks and these indicate that a character is speaking. Point out to the students that they will also encounter an em dash in the second, fifth, and sixth stanzas. Remind them that an em dash indicates a pause.

Develop Oral Language
Have students work in groups of six to read the poem. Invite each student to read one of the stanzas.

Writing

Have students use the KWHL chart from page 9 to organize information for a historical narrative verse. Challenge students to work in groups to write information about a famous person in history. After they have completed the chart, have them write about the person.

Name _____   Date _____

[from] Paul Revere's Ride
by Henry Wadsworth Longfellow

Listen, my children, and you shall hear
Of the midnight ride of Paul Revere,
On the eighteenth of April, in Seventy-five;
Hardly a man is now alive
Who remembers that famous day and year.

He said to his friend, "If the British march
By land or sea from the town to-night,
Hang a lantern aloft in the belfry arch
Of the North Church tower as a signal light,—
One, if by land, and two, if by sea;
And I on the opposite shore will be,
Ready to ride and spread the alarm
Through every Middlesex village and farm
For the country folk to be up and to arm."
....

Meanwhile, impatient to mount and ride,
Booted and spurred, with a heavy stride
On the opposite shore walked Paul Revere.
Now he patted his horse's side,
Now gazed at the landscape far and near,
Then, impetuous, stamped the earth,
And turned and tightened his saddle-girth;
But mostly he watched with eager search
The belfry-tower of the Old North Church,
As it rose above the graves on the hill,
Lonely and spectral and sombre and still.
And lo! as he looks, on the belfry's height
A glimmer, and then a gleam of light!
He springs to the saddle, the bridle he turns,
But lingers and gazes, till full on his sight
A second lamp in the belfry burns!
....

It was two by the village clock,
When he came to the bridge in Concord town.
He heard the bleating of the flock,
And the twitter of birds among the trees,
And felt the breath of the morning breeze
Blowing over the meadows brown.
And one was safe and asleep in his bed
Who at the bridge would be first to fall,
Who that day would be lying dead,
Pierced by a British musket-ball.

You know the rest. In the books you have read,
How the British Regulars fired and fled,—
How the farmers gave them ball for ball,
From behind each fence and farm-yard wall,
Chasing the red-coats down the lane,
Then crossing the fields to emerge again
Under the trees at the turn of the road,
And only pausing to fire and load.

So through the night rode Paul Revere;
And so through the night went his cry of alarm
To every Middlesex village and farm,—
A cry of defiance and not of fear,
A voice in the darkness, a knock at the door,
And a word that shall echo forevermore!
For, borne on the night-wind of the Past,
Through all our history, to the last,
In the hour of darkness and peril and need,
The people will waken and listen to hear
The hurrying hoof-beats of that steed,
And the midnight message of Paul Revere.

87

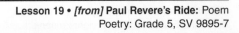

[from] **Paul Revere's Ride:** Assessment

Think about the poem. Then answer the questions. Fill in the circle next to the correct answer.

1. Paul Revere warned the people that
   Ⓐ the Americans were coming.
   Ⓑ the villagers were sleeping.
   Ⓒ the British were coming.
   Ⓓ the British were sailing away.

2. What did Paul's friend do before Paul rode off?
   Ⓐ He hung a lamp in the church tower.
   Ⓑ He shouted to Paul to go.
   Ⓒ He sent a messenger across the river to Paul.
   Ⓓ He hung two lamps in the church tower.

3. In the poem, the people are "Chasing the red-coats down the lane,/Then crossing the fields to emerge again." "Emerge" means
   Ⓐ go back.
   Ⓑ enter.
   Ⓒ come out.
   Ⓓ run off.

4. The poem is mostly about
   Ⓐ what good friends can do for each other.
   Ⓑ how one man made a difference in history.
   Ⓒ why horses are important for transportation.
   Ⓓ how to send a message across water.

5. If Paul Revere had not made his ride,
   Ⓐ the British may have defeated the Americans.
   Ⓑ the British would not have been able to fight.
   Ⓒ the Americans would have been caught by surprise.
   Ⓓ both A. and C.

6. Paul Revere was probably
   Ⓐ timid and hesitant.
   Ⓑ wild and careless.
   Ⓒ patriotic and brave.
   Ⓓ young and foolish.

7. How would Paul Revere know the British were coming?

   _____

   _____

   _____

www.harcourtschoolsupply.com
 88
Lesson 19 • [from] **Paul Revere's Ride:** Poem Assessment
Poetry: Grade 5, SV 9895-7

Base Words

Base words are words without any endings or other word parts added to them. Some endings are **ing, d, ed, s,** and **es**. Sometimes the spelling of the base word changes when an ending is added to it.

    Examples: remember—remembers   flame—flaming

Read each base word. Add <u>ing</u>, <u>d</u>, <u>ed</u>, <u>s</u>, or <u>es</u> to each base word to make a new word. Use your new word in a sentence. Use a dictionary for help with spelling.

1. arm _____

_____

2. emerge _____

_____

3. stride _____

_____

4. peril _____

_____

Write the base word of each word below. Then, use the base word in a sentence.

5. bleating _____

_____

6. lingers _____

_____

Lesson 19 • *[from]* **Paul Revere's Ride:** Vocabulary Skill
Poetry: Grade 5, SV 9895-7

[from] The Spider and the Fly

Standard
Identify the use of figurative language (personification)

Explore Personification
Explain to students that poets use personification to give human qualities to an animal or an object. In this poem, Mary Howitt gave the spider and the fly the human qualities of speech, thought, and feelings. Have students look for descriptive words that give human qualities to the spider and the fly. Have students write these descriptive words on a word web for each animal.

Vocabulary

alas–an exclamation of sorrow or great sadness
affection–a tender feeling toward another; fondness
cunning–clever in deceiving or tricking
dismal–dark and gloomy
flattering–praising too much or beyond truth
flitting–flying lightly and quickly from one place to another
hither–to this place
sly–tricky or crafty in a mean way; cunning
subtle–finely woven and difficult to see
vain–without success
wily–full of tricks

Summary

This well-known poem is about a "wily" spider who preys upon an innocent and somewhat vain fly. The spider very carefully lures the fly into his "parlor" by flattering her.

Read the Poem

Introduce the Poem
Ask students about picture books that they remember reading when they were younger. Have them share the titles of the ones that they loved to read over and over again. Introduce this poem by using one of the picture book versions of this poem. Instead of reading the whole poem at first, give a "Book Review."

Introduce the Vocabulary
Write the vocabulary words and the definitions on separate cards. Put them in a pocket chart in any order. Say a sentence with a vocabulary word and ask a volunteer to find the word and its definition.

After Reading

Activity
Remind students that a poem can tell a story in the same way a book can. The poem can describe characters and have a setting, a problem, and events that lead to a solution. Use the story map from page 13 to map the story.

Fluency
Explain that the poem has lots of end punctuation. Model how to read the first stanza of the poem, discussing the punctuation as you encounter it. Then have partners rehearse the poem several times.

Develop Oral Language
Have partners alternate reading the verses. Challenge students to practice reading this poem as a play. Have one student take the part of the fly and have the other take the part of the spider. Encourage students to use inflection in their voices to show the difference between the two characters.

Writing

Have the students continue to work as partners. Using "The Spider and the Fly" as a model, have them use the story map from page 13 to write a poem of their own. Encourage students to choose two different animals to write about. Remind them to give their animal characters human qualities.

Name _____   Date _____

[from] The Spider and the Fly
by Mary Howitt

"Will you walk into my parlor?" said the spider to the fly;
"'Tis the prettiest parlor that ever you did spy.
The way into my parlor is up a winding stair,
And I have many pretty things to show when you are there."

"O, no, no," said the little fly, "to ask me is in vain,
For who goes up your winding stair can never come down again."

Said the cunning spider to the fly, "Dear friend, what shall I do
To prove the warm affection I've always felt for you?
I have within my pantry good store of all that's nice;
I'm sure you're very welcome. Will you please to take a slice?"

"O, no, no," said the little fly, "kind sir, that cannot be,
I've heard what's in your pantry, and I do not wish to see."

The spider turned him 'round about and went into his den,
For well he knew the silly fly would soon be back again:
So he wove a subtle web in a little corner sly,
And set his table ready to dine upon the fly.
Then he came out to his door again, and merrily did sing,
"Come hither, hither, pretty fly, with pearl and silver wing:
Your robes are green and purple: there's a crest upon your head;
Your eyes are like the diamond bright, but mine are dull as lead."

Alas, alas! How very soon this silly little fly,
Hearing his wily flattering words, came slowly flitting by.
Up jumped the cunning spider, and fiercely held her fast.
He dragged her up his winding stair, into his dismal den,
Within his little parlor; but she never came out again!

Understand the Poem

[from] The Spider and the Fly: Assessment

Think about the poem. Then answer the questions. Fill in the circle next to the correct answer.

1. The spider invites the fly to
- Ⓐ sit and visit for a while.
- Ⓑ come see all of the pretty things in his parlor.
- Ⓒ weave a web with him.
- Ⓓ slide down his "winding stair."

2. What did the spider do after the fly refused his invitation to eat with him?
- Ⓐ He tried to follow her.
- Ⓑ He spun a web in a corner.
- Ⓒ He offered her food again.
- Ⓓ He left her alone.

3. What is the meaning of "cunning" in the poem?
- Ⓐ honest
- Ⓑ friendly
- Ⓒ tricky
- Ⓓ frightened

4. The poet's message in this poem is
- Ⓐ that neighbors should keep to themselves.
- Ⓑ that you should never go into a stranger's house.
- Ⓒ that you should not always trust others just because they give you praise and compliments.
- Ⓓ that flies shouldn't be friends with spiders.

5. Without all of the spider's flattery,
- Ⓐ the fly would be hungry.
- Ⓑ the fly would escape from the spider's parlor.
- Ⓒ the fly would still be alive.
- Ⓓ the fly would have stopped to visit with the spider.

6. The spider will probably
- Ⓐ be satisfied with his meal.
- Ⓑ use his flattery to lure some other fly into his web.
- Ⓒ feel depressed that he has no one to talk to.
- Ⓓ be kinder to insects.

7. Is this story real or make-believe? How do you know?

_____

_____

www.harcourtschoolsupply.com
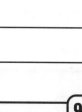 92
Lesson 20 • [from] The Spider and the Fly: Poem Assessment
Poetry: Grade 5, SV 9895-7

Name _____   Date _____

Antonyms

Antonyms are words with opposite meanings.
    Examples: loss—gain   never—always

✎ **Match the words in the box with their antonyms listed below. Write the words on the line.**

| dull   winding   flattering   affection   vain   dismal   subtle   sly |

_____   **1.** insulting

_____   **2.** honest

_____   **3.** interesting

_____   **4.** dislike

_____   **5.** straight

_____   **6.** successful

_____   **7.** obvious

_____   **8.** bright

Dictionary Skills

The words in a dictionary are listed in **alphabetical order**.
    Example: read, school, spelling, success

✎ **Write the vocabulary words from the box above in alphabetical order.**

9. _____   _____

    _____   _____

    _____   _____

    _____   _____

Lesson 20 • *[from]* The Spider and the Fly: Vocabulary Skill
Poetry: Grade 5, SV 9895-7

Poetry Grade 5 • Answer Key

Page 8
1. B
2. A
3. D
4. A
5. D
6. C
7. The child will not answer him.

Page 16
1. A
2. C
3. B
4. D
5. B
6. A
7. Possible responses: Candy and food grow on plants. You can eat whatever you want, whenever you want. No one will interrupt your play.

Page 17
Across
2. scamper
4. damper
5. whither
Down
1. naught
2. sapient
3. romping

Page 20
1. C
2. D
3. A
4. C
5. D
6. B
7. Possible response: The poet goes from a quiet, reflective mood in haikus #1 and #2 to an excited mood in haiku #3.

Page 21
1. renewing
2. quenching
3. depth
4. rippling
5. breaks
6. anxiously

Page 24
1. D
2. C
3. A
4. C
5. C
6. B
7. Answers will vary.

Page 25
1. smokestack
2. steamboat
3. cottonfields
4. lowland

Page 28
1. B
2. D
3. A
4. C
5. B
6. D
7. to contrast two opposite nouns or things

Page 29
1. G
2. D
3. F
4. C
5. H
6. E
7. A
8. B
9. Sentences will vary.

Page 32
1. C
2. C
3. A
4. B
5. C
6. B
7. He meant that everyone showed a reaction by doing something (Timothy took a picture, gardener laughed, ducks quacked).

Page 33
1. dismal
2. complained
3. merry
4. respond
5. quickly
6. daft

Page 36
1. C
2. A
3. B
4. B
5. A
6. C
7. This is a free verse poem because it does not rhyme.

Page 37
Pictures and sentences will vary.

Page 40
1. D
2. A
3. B
4. C
5. C
6. A
7. He was trying to tell the reader that his parents saw him and quickly sent him to bed.

Page 41
1. B
2. A
3. B
4. A
5. B
6. A

Page 44
1. B
2. D
3. D
4. A
5. B
6. C
7. The snow is melted except for what is left on top of the hill.

94

www.harcourtschoolsupply.com
© Harcourt Achieve Inc. All rights reserved.

Answer Key
Poetry: Grade 5, SV 9895-7

Poetry Grade 5 • Answer Key

Page 45
1. retreated
2. never
3. bare
4. small
5. prevailing
6. joy
7. defeated
8. oldest
Sentences will vary.

Page 48
1. B
2. B
3. D
4. C
5. D
6. B
7. Possible response: They have no need for tears because even though he is dead, he had a good life with them. They have the memories of him.

Page 49
1. pity
2. region
3. graven
4. sorrow
5. mournful
6. among
7. death
8. traveler
Sentences will vary.

Page 52
1. D
2. A
3. C
4. B
5. A
6. C
7. Answers will vary; however, they should reflect that she can tell how she feels and what she thinks.

Page 53
1. F
2. G
3. A
4. B
5. E
6. C
7. D
8. H
9. Sentences will vary.

Page 56
1. A
2. C
3. D
4. D
5. C
6. A
7. Possible responses: He hopes his son will continue to dream and have goals. He does not want him to stop dreaming of all the possibilities.

Page 57
1. A
2. B
3. C
4. A
5. B

Page 60
1. B
2. C
3. A
4. D
5. A
6. C
7. Answers may vary. Possible responses: He always got into trouble because he was expected to get into trouble. He always got into trouble because he was angry with others and did things that he should not to get even with them. He might have even been blamed for things he didn't really do.

Page 61
Students should write the sentences, using these words:
1. I am
2. against
3. it was
4. They have
5. it is, that is

Page 64
1. B
2. D
3. C
4. D
5. C
6. A
7. The poet probably chose the title because it indicates that this is a special time he spends with his children daily.

Page 65
Order of answers may vary on 1.–6. Answers to check for are: daylight, lamplight, stairway, overjoyed, everywhere, forever
7.–12. Alphabetical order: daylight, everywhere, forever, lamplight, overjoyed, stairway

Page 68
1. A
2. C
3. B
4. D
5. C
6. D
7. The mother is really telling the son not to become weak and not to give up when things seem hard.

Page 69
Students should write the sentences, using these words:
1. I will
2. reaching
3. It is
4. Do not
5. going

Poetry Grade 5 • Answer Key

Page 72
1. C
2. B
3. D
4. B
5. C
6. A
7. This sentence is a simile because it is comparing two things and uses the word *like*.

Page 73
Across
2. sunning
4. portrait
5. chimney
Down
1. borrowed
3. neighbor
6. meadow

Page 76
1. D
2. A
3. C
4. A
5. B
6. C
7. This line shows a transition or change in the mood of the poem. The people are being saved and their anguish turns to joy.

Page 77
1. hero
2. fate
3. crown
4. yield
5. rage
6. help
Sentences will vary.

Page 80
1. A
2. D
3. C
4. C
5. B
6. C
7. Longfellow appeals to your sense of hearing by describing things you can hear.

Page 81
1. C
2. G
3. B or F
4. F or B
5. A
6. D
7. E
8.–14. Sentences will vary.

Page 84
1. B
2. B
3. D
4. B
5. A
6. C
7. Possible response: The people did not think the flower was beautiful because it was unusual. They were not used to seeing it and there were only a few of them. Once many of them grew, seeing them in mass made it more beautiful. The people got used to the flower.

Page 85
1. cast
2. discontent
3. muttered
4. crown
5. splendid
6. poor

Page 88
1. C
2. D
3. C
4. B
5. D
6. C
7. A lantern in the North Church tower would signal that the British were coming. One lantern would show they were coming by land and two lanterns would show they were coming by water.

Page 89
Answers may vary on 1.–4. Possible answers:
1. arms, armed, arming
2. emerges, emerged, emerging
3. strides, striding
4. perils, periled
5. bleat
6. linger
Sentences for 1.–6. will vary.

Page 92
1. B
2. B
3. C
4. C
5. C
6. B
7. This is a make-believe story. It is make-believe because the spider and the fly can talk.

Page 93
1. flattering
2. sly
3. dull
4. affection
5. winding
6. vain
7. subtle
8. dismal
9. Alphabetical order: affection, dismal, dull, flattering, sly, subtle, vain, winding

Reference
Fountas, Irene C. and Pinnell, Gay Su. 2001. *Guiding Readers and Writers: Grades 3–6.* Portsmouth, NH: Heinemann.

Poetry: Grade 5, SV 9895-7